D1039379

God the Evangelist

How the Holy Spirit Works to Bring Men and Women to Faith

David F. Wells

William B. Eerdmans • *Grand Rapids*
The Paternoster Press • *Exeter*

This edition published 1987 by Wm. B. Eerdmans
Publishing Co. on behalf of the Lausanne
Committee for World Evangelization and the
World Evangelical Fellowship.

Library of Congress Cataloging-in-Publication Data

Wells, David F.
God the evangelist.

Bibliography: p. 124
1. Holy Spirit — Congresses.   2. Evangelistic work —
Congresses.   I. Title.
BT121.2.W45   1987   231'.3   87-6733

ISBN 0-8028-0271-0

British Library Cataloguing-in-Publication Data

Wells, David F.

God the evangelist: how the Holy Spirit works to
bring men and women to faith.
I. Holy Spirit
1. Title
231'.3   T C   121.1

ISBN 0 85364 455 1

ι

Contents

To
all of God's people who
labor in obscurity,
suffer in poverty, or
live in contexts of violence

Preface

The Consultation on the Work of the Holy Spirit and Evangelization was held at the Intermission Bible School in Oslo, Norway, in May 1985. It was sponsored by the Theology Working Group of the Lausanne Committee for World Evangelization and the Theology Unit of the World Evangelical Fellowship. Dr. Tormod Engelsviken was the coordinator, and a number of churches and Christian organizations gave generous support to the undertaking.

The Consultation was relatively small: it consisted of forty-six participants, who represented all continents, many denominations, and both charismatic and noncharismatic churches. Among them were evangelists, theologians, pastors, and church leaders. In addition, there were fifteen observers who were able to make valuable contributions. Certain participants were invited because they were able to provide remarkable case studies of the Holy Spirit's work in evangelization.

We participants spent the first day examining the doctrine of the Holy Spirit in the Scriptures and went on to explore three great themes: the Holy Spirit in relation to creation and history, the Holy Spirit empowering the local church for evangelization, and the Holy Spirit confronting the world. Papers had been circulated before the Consultation, and debate and discussion took place on each issue. The importance of the topic became clearer each day, and we constantly reiterated our wish to understand the Holy Spirit's work in relation to evangelism. The place of signs and wonders in the communication of the Good News was a matter of special inquiry. We did not always resolve our differences, but the value of consulting together in face-to-face discussion was reinforced again and again.

It should be recorded that on the second-to-last day, we broke away from our prearranged agenda to spend time in prayer together. That time proved to be one of the most memorable parts of the Consultation; it gave us a confirming assurance of the presence of the Spirit.

We had no doubt that the results of the Consultation should be shared with the people of God. This Consultation was held not merely for the private benefit of the participants but to further interest in the Holy Spirit's work throughout the church. A book, it was decided, would be the best vehicle for fulfilling this obligation.

But the Consultation had to confront two major difficulties in this regard. First, what it had in hand was a number of papers that by themselves did not constitute a uniform, rounded statement of the Holy Spirit's work. Second, much that happened during the Consultation took the collective understanding of the participants beyond the papers with which they had started. We therefore decided to ask David Wells to write an account of this subject that would utilize the papers as sources, put the material in as orderly a form as possible, and include the benefits of the discussions and exchanges wherever he judged these to be appropriate.

The result is this book, of which David Wells is both editor and author. Inasmuch as he has contributed material to it and structured the materials he was given, he is the author. He has given his own interpretation of the Consultation, and thus not every participant will necessarily agree with every sentence. But he has, of course, worked conscientiously with an editorial committee and has sought to be fair to all the participants. Insofar as he functioned as an editor, he utilized and built upon the work of others. The list of contributors is a long one: James Packer ("The New Testament Witness to the Holy Spirit"); Oskar Skarsaune ("The Life-giving Spirit: Some Aspects of Pneumatology in the Old Church" and "The Doctrine of the Spirit: The Augustinian Heritage in the Middle Ages and in the Reformation"); Robert Godfrey ("Reformed Thought on the Work of the Holy Spirit and Evangelization: An Historical Overview"); William Menzies ("The Development of Spirit Theology: A Pentecostal Perspective" and "The Work of the Spirit in Preparing People for the Gospel"); Hans-Jürgen Peters ("The Rediscovery of Teaching about the Holy Spirit in Missiology"); Tormod Engelsviken ("The Work of the Spirit in Creation and History"); Peter Kuzmic ("The Spirit, the Kingdom and the Church"); John Reid ("The Holy Spirit Empowering in the Local Church for Evangelization"); Klaus Bockmuehl ("Renewed Life-style"); Colin Buchanan ("Renewal of Congregational Life and Ministry"); Gottfried Osei-Mensah ("Renewal in Fellowship and Unity in the Body of Christ"); Leighton Ford ("The Holy Spirit in Evangelistic Ministry"); Ada Lum ("Evangelistic Bible Studies: A Universal Tool"); John Wimber ("The Holy Spirit and Personal Evangelism"); Roberta Hestenes ("Personal Spirituality and World Evangelization"); Henri Blocher ("The Work of the Spirit and the New Life in Christ"); David Cook ("The Work of the Holy Spirit towards the World"); Detmar Scheunemann ("The Work of the Holy Spirit Equipping the Church to Face the Demonic, Supernatural Powers of the World"); Bruce Nicholls ("The Holy Spirit Confronts the World of Religions"); Myung Hyuk Kim ("Can Revivals

Be Prepared for by Man or Are They Created by God?"); Caesar Mole-
batsi ("Urban Evangelism in a Context of Division and Conflict"); Alan
Cole ("Signs and Wonders"); Olof Djurfeldt ("The Use of Modern Theology in Evangelization"); and Knud Jørgensen ("The Use of Electronic
Media in Evangelization"). In addition, a number of case studies detail-
ing the Holy Spirit's work in various places in the world were produced
by Robert Crandall, Alan Cole, Gresford Chitemo, Iteffa Gobena, Jannes
Hasselhorn, Philip LeFeuvre, and Eric Mayer.

The creation of this book has therefore been unusual. It bears testimony to the sense of obligation that we feel to the church, the urgency
with which we want to raise afresh the issues that are here addressed. And
it is also an impressive witness to the growing desire among evangelicals
to unite in the common cause of making known Christ's saving work. It is
sent forth with a heartfelt desire that the Holy Spirit, whose presence was
very evident in the Consultation, will fall afresh on us all, and that power
will be given to God's people to preach the Good News with effectiveness.

JOHN R. REID
Chairman of the Consultation

Introduction

On Being Serious about the Holy Spirit

J. I. Packer

These pages are a sort of hors d'oeuvres. They are meant to whet your appetite for David Wells's digest of the substance and significance of the Oslo Consultation on the Work of the Holy Spirit and Evangelization.

What happened in that Consultation may have been momentous; time will tell. Certainly it felt significant as it happened. A wealth of Third World vision and experience in evangelism was shared with stiff-jointed and perhaps stiff-necked Westerners. Pentecostal and charismatic evangelicals were effectively welded into fellowship with those of an older cultural type. Material was provided for evaluating the emphasis on "signs and wonders" in evangelism. The Holy Spirit himself did much for us, corporately and individually, during a half-morning of prayer together. It was a privilege to be part of the Oslo experience.

The Consultation sought to take the Holy Spirit seriously in connection with evangelism, and this to me was a further sign of that widening and deepening concern to take the Holy Spirit seriously in all realms of life, a concern that is one of the most hopeful developments of our time. It is on this development as a whole that I want to comment now, in the hope that my comments may help to focus Oslo's long-term significance.

Forty years ago, when I was a theological student, little was said or written about the Holy Spirit—so little that he was sometimes referred to as the displaced person of the Godhead and the Cinderella of theology. Apart from evangelical exponents of what was then called holiness teaching in its various forms, no one seemed interested in the subject. That has changed: Trinitarian thinking has revived among theologians, charismatic renewal has touched and challenged the whole Christian world, and aspects of the doctrine of the Spirit are nowadays frequently discussed.

Yet one may still ask, Do we take the Spirit seriously enough? I fear that, whoever we are and whatever our heritage, the answer is often no. Let me explain.

The first thing to say is that for a long time it has been hard for Protestants to reckon seriously with the Holy Spirit because, however ardent their hearts, the depersonalized, nonregenerative pneumatology of classic liberalism has throttled their thoughts.

The liberal habit was and is to reduce the Trinity to a threefoldness in our perception of God—God above, beside, and within us; to reduce the Incarnation to a special case of divine influence in a human life; and to reduce the Spirit to a name for the unipersonal God in action—if, indeed, the liberal thinker is willing to speak of God as personal at all. Within this frame of reference, the explicit New Testament teaching about the Spirit's personhood and personal ministry cannot be affirmed. Furthermore, liberalism has habitually identified the Spirit's renewing work with some form of cultural transformation—evolutionary or revolutionary—in human society, as opposed to the regenerative transformation of individuals brought to know Jesus Christ; and this identification has constantly obstructed the necessary assertion that God's basic method of changing society is to change the individuals who compose it. The Holy Spirit is not and cannot be taken seriously as long as he is thought of in the liberal way.

The second thing to say is that for an even longer period, Christians have failed to take the Holy Spirit seriously because they have institutionalized him.

The Holy Spirit is institutionalized the moment that God's people, on whatever grounds, allow themselves to assume that their own current practice is a guaranteed vehicle of his presence and power. Protestants have often censured Roman Catholics for making this assumption about the sacramental ministrations of their priests, as if the claimed apostolic succession of orders (supposing, for the moment, that this is fact and not fable) could in principle guarantee such a thing. But when Protestants continue unconcerned in church situations unmarked by changed lives, joy in worship, and zeal in witness, they show themselves to be falling into the same trap and making an identical mistake. When churches treat any of their characteristics—their orthodoxy, their separated stance, their loyalty to traditional expressions of faith, their up-to-dateness in worship, their charismatic ethos and routines, their interest in "signs and wonders," or their opposition to cooperative evangelism and Geneva-based ecumenism—as guaranteeing that the Spirit will be with them to bless them, irrespective of whether or not experience bears them out, they are institutionalizing the Spirit. They are making the same mistake if they look to their own good organization and administration, alluring programs, stockpiled counseling skills, and ecclesiastical expertise in general as constituting sufficient proof that God is with them, and if they compile statistics, issue reports, and hire pastors on that basis. The truth is that any church can institutionalize the Spirit by becoming triumphalist and complacent. By resting on their oars, churches settle on their lees. Ecclesiastical formalism sets in, and the Spirit is institutionalized with disastrous consequences.

For the Holy Spirit's true work is to lead sinners to Christ and through Christ to God; to make individual believers Christ-like in love, humility, righteousness, and patience; and to animate the church corporately to offer praise to God, service and help to each other, and compassionate outreach to the world. Institutionalizing the Spirit in the way described makes for apathy and indifference to spiritual quality so long as the ecclesiastical machine rolls on. This obstructs church growth in Paul's sense of the phrase—that is, corporate advance toward the fullness of Christ (Eph. 4:15-16; Col. 2:19)—and thus quenches the Spirit by not taking him seriously. Complacency is the cause, and Laodicean lukewarmness the consequence.

The third thing to say is that taking the Holy Spirit seriously means that Christians must rediscover the naturalness of three things that modern believers in the West rarely see as natural—namely, worship, evangelism, and suffering.

With regard to worship, A. W. Tozer wrote in 1948,

> There are today many millions of people who hold "right opinions," probably more than ever before in the history of the Church. Yet I wonder if there was ever a time when true spiritual worship was at a lower ebb. To great sections of the Church the art of worship has been lost entirely, and in its place has come that strange and foreign thing called the "program." This word has been borrowed from the stage and applied with sad wisdom to the type of public service which now passes for worship among us.

This is arguably truer now than it was when Tozer wrote about it. Worship—in the sense of telling God his worth by speech and song and celebrating his worth in his presence by proclamation and meditation—has been largely replaced, at least in the West, by a form of entertainment calculated to give worshipers the equivalent of a sauna or Jacuzzi experience and send them away feeling relaxed and tuned up at the same time. Certainly true worship invigorates, but to plan invigoration is not necessarily to order worship. As all that glitters is not gold, so all that makes us feel happy and strong is not worship. The question is not whether a particular liturgical form is used, but whether a God-centered as distinct from a man-centered perspective is maintained—whether, in other words, the sense that man exists for God rather than God for man is cherished or lost. We need to discover all over again that worship is natural to the Christian heart, as it was to the godly Israelites who wrote the psalms, and that the habit of celebrating the greatness and graciousness of God yields an endless flow of thankfulness, joy, and zeal. Neither stylized charismatic exuberance nor Anglican Prayer Book correctness nor conventional music-sandwich Sunday-morning programs provide any magic formula for this rediscovery. It can occur only when the Holy Spirit is taken seriously as the One who through the written word of Scripture shows us the love and glory of the Son and the Father and draws us into personal communion with both.

Harry S. Boer wrote tellingly of the naturalness of evangelism in *Pentecost and Missions*. There he showed that the view of evangelism as first and foremost a Christian duty required by the Great Commission of Matthew 28:19-20 is no older than the last century, prior to which the mainspring of evangelism among lay Christians was the naturalness of sharing Christ with one's neighbor out of sheer inner excitement over the new life of hope one had found. Thus it was in Jerusalem after Pentecost. Thus it was for three centuries after that, during which Christianity, though it was legally proscribed and its adherents were often killed, became the strongest religion in the Roman Empire—so strong that it can truly be said to have won the Western world. Thus it was in the day of the Reformers, in the time of the Puritans, and during the evangelical awakenings that revived faith on both sides of the Atlantic in the eighteenth century. In those eras the gospel spread like a prairie fire, not primarily because of the quality of the preachers but because lay Christians kept gossiping the gospel to their neighbors. And they did so spontaneously, simply because they had been thrilled to the marrow by their own experience of God's salvation, which had made them into conscious lovers of Christ and heirs of heaven, no longer victims and prisoners of the pains and pressures—physical and mental, secular and religious—that threatened them on earth.

But during the past century Christians have become unbiblically and indeed pathetically earthbound, concentrating their hopes of happiness on the here rather than the hereafter. And as the glow of the hope of glory has faded, credibility has diminished, and zeal for sharing Christ has waned. Meantime, evangelism has been institutionalized in various forms and programs of organized mission activity, thus becoming a duty rather than a delight. Paul prayed for the Romans, "May the God of hope fill you with all joy and peace as you trust in him, so that you may overflow with hope by the power of the Holy Spirit" (15:13). Only as the Holy Spirit is taken seriously enough for this overflowing to become a reality in our own lives will the naturalness of evangelism be discovered again.

As for suffering, by which I mean all forms of pain, frustration, and disappointment—"losses and crosses," as the Puritans used to put it—the New Testament is consistent and emphatic in viewing this as the natural condition of Christians and churches as long as they are in this world. We follow Christ through humiliation here, sharing his sufferings, and thus arrive at glorification with him hereafter. Afflictions achieve "an eternal glory that far outweighs them all," Paul tells us (2 Cor. 4:17), while the alternative, in William Penn's haunting phrase, is "no cross, no crown" (see Heb. 12:7-14). Suffering is the Christian's road home; no other road leads there. But the twentieth-century West has come to think of a life free from pain and trouble as virtually a natural human right, and Christian minds have been so swamped by this thinking that nowadays any pain and loss in a Christian's life is felt to cast doubt on God's goodness. It is perhaps no wonder that our age has produced the gospel of health and wealth, promising that God will give us right now whatever we name and claim under either heading; no wonder, either, that the triumphs of the "power encounter" between the Christ of the Gospels and the secular and satanic forces that he faces should be equated by some with supernatural healings of the physical body rather than with supernatural transformations of the moral character. But if we can learn to take the Holy Spirit seriously once more, he will convince us afresh of the naturalness of suffering in the Christian life, probably by leading us into a higher degree of it than we have yet had to face.

It seems that at this point in history the burden of evangelizing and planting churches worldwide, wherever doors remain open, rests upon the shoulders of evangelicals who recognize in the Lausanne Covenant God's marching orders for mission. Other Christian constituencies seem for practical purposes to have abandoned this task. Humankind's need and evangelical responsibility are both great, and the call to take the Holy Spirit seriously, as the renewer of God's people and the empowerer of their witness, was never more urgent. The Consultation that produced this book and the book itself should be seen as pointers in the direction in which, please God, we shall all soon find ourselves moving. For the word that bears on our unfinished task, as on Zerubbabel's long ago, is "'Not by might nor by power, but by my Spirit,' says the Lord Almighty" (Zech. 4:6). God help us to hear it!

Chapter I

Spirit of the Living God

Christian faith in New Testament times is inexplicable without reference to the Holy Spirit; indeed, without his presence and power, his illumination and transformation, faith in any age is without explanation. Not only so, but without his work, the Incarnation and Resurrection of Christ would not have occurred as recorded, the Scriptures would not have been given as we have them, regeneration could not occur as we have experienced it, and the gospel could not be preached with any assurance that in it is God's power by which fallen sinners are reconciled to him.

And yet, despite all of this, the Holy Spirit is an enigma in contemporary theology. Those theologians who have constructed their theology outside of the authoritative functioning of Scripture are often disinclined to see him as part of the Trinity. From the time of Schleiermacher at the beginning of the last century to the present, the currents of unitarianism have been strong. Thus "Holy Spirit" has often been seen as just another name for God in action, or perhaps as a synonym for God's power, but not as the name of a distinct, eternal, and self-conscious member of the Godhead. As the identity of the Holy Spirit has eroded and then crumbled, questions have arisen about the nature of his work. The most important development here has been the breakdown of the Spirit's relation to the Cross and the redemptive purposes of Christ.

In historic Christian thought, the work of Christ has been seen to gain us the status of children of God, and the work of the Spirit has been viewed as giving us that experience. There has been a unity between what Christ did and what the Spirit now does. Christ died for sinners; the Holy Spirit regenerates Christ's people, his bride, constituting them as the church, filling, transforming, and empowering them. It is no surprise to find that in the New Testament the Holy Spirit is not merely referred to as the Spirit of God but is frequently spoken of as the "Spirit of Christ." He is the other Paraclete (John 14:16) whose work grows out of, is centered upon, and returns to the Christ who sent him. It is not possible to separate Christ's work in his people from the Spirit's. The connection between the person and work of Christ and the person and work of the Spirit is everywhere present in the epistles of the New Testament. It is a bond at once indissoluble and essential, for the Spirit is our link to the historic Jesus through whom alone sin is forgiven and the world is overcome.

This bond, however, has frequently been severed in contemporary theology. The Spirit's work is cut loose from that of the historic Jesus. Most commonly, God is seen to be working throughout humanity, and often in non-Christian religions. Any expression of truth in these religions is thought to be the result of the "Spirit's" work. The "Spirit," therefore, becomes equated with the human spirit. Wherever higher values appear in human life, we can point to the "Spirit's" presence. In some liberation theologies, for example, the struggle for justice in contexts of oppression is directly ascribed to the Spirit, for the presence of God is seen to be registering in those social eruptions in which what is wrong is overthrown. Syncretism such as we have in Africa, as well as the more complex movement toward a synthesis of world religions favored in some Western academic circles, is usually explained in a similar way.

But to speak of the Spirit's work in this way is to cut it loose from the known and declared objectives of Christ's death. It is to evacuate the Spirit's work of salvific intent, in New Testament terms at least, and it is to substitute the world for the church as his primary locus of work. We thus stand on its head the prayer of John 17, in which Jesus explicitly limited his saving design to his people and declined to pray for the world. We also make redundant what Jesus did on the Cross. In the name of the Spirit we belie the mission of Christ!

Is it any surprise, then, that confusion about the Holy Spirit has produced confusion about Christian faith? Reconstructions of the doctrine of the Holy Spirit have produced reconstructions of those doctrines directly related to the Spirit. The doctrine of our triune God, the person and work of the Christ, the nature and function of Scripture, the content of the gospel, the nature and boundaries of the church, the meaning and means of Christian living—all have been drastically affected. If we misunderstand the Bible's teaching on the Spirit, we will misunderstand its teaching on all of these other matters. Our knowledge of God will be vitiated, and our ability to understand his world aright will be destroyed.

The Holy Spirit in the Old Testament

In considering the person of the Spirit, we need to begin with the Old Testament, for the New builds upon it. The New Testament proclaims the fulfillment in Christ of the principles, prophecies, and hopes of the Old Testament. It proclaims the Old Testament as Christian Scripture, Scripture that is written to instruct Christians in the knowledge and service of God and yields up its deepest meaning only to them (Rom. 15:4; 1 Cor. 10:11; 2 Cor. 3:14-18; 2 Tim. 3:15-17; 1 Pet. 1:10-12; 2 Pet. 1:19-21; 3:16; cf. Heb. 10:15). In this sense, then, the New is hidden in the Old, and the Old is fulfilled in the New. This means that the Old Testament lays a foundation on which the New builds, but it does not necessarily mean that the Old should have meanings read into it from the New. We need, therefore, to prepare ourselves to see a development in the doctrine of the Holy Spirit as we move from one testament to the other.

There are just under one hundred explicit references to the Spirit in the Old Testament. "Spirit" is usually expressed by *ruach*. This is a word that is used of wind, usually wind in motion, or of the breath in people and animals. It signifies power that is let loose, energy that is being exercised.

This power and this energy, which are the very power and energy of God himself, were expressed in seven main functions of the Spirit. First, we see it in creation in the way God shaped animate beings and the cosmos (Gen. 1:2; 2:7; cf. Ps. 33:6; Job 26:13; 33:4). Second, it is evident in the control of nature and history (Ps. 104:29-30; Isa. 34:16; 40:7). Third, it was by this Spirit that God's truth was revealed and his will was made known (Num. 24:2; 2 Sam. 23:2; 2 Chron. 12:18; 15:1; Neh. 9:30; Job 32:8; Isa. 61:1-4; Ezek. 2:2; 11:24; 37:1; Mic. 3:8; Zech. 7:12). Fourth, by these revelations the Spirit taught God's people the way of faithfulness and fruitfulness (Neh. 9:20; Ps. 143:10; Isa. 48:16; 63:10-14). Fifth, it is this power that elicited personal response to God in the form of faith, repentance, obedience, righteousness, openness to God's instructions, and fellowship with him through praise and prayer (Ps. 51:10-12; Isa. 11:2; 44:3; Ezek. 11:19; 36:25-27; 37:14; 39:29; Joel 2:28-29; Zech. 12:10). Sixth, this Spirit equipped people for leadership (Gen. 41:38; Num. 11:16-29; 27:18; Deut. 34:9; Judg. 3:10; 6:34; 11:29; 13:25; 14:19; 15:14; 1 Sam. 10:10; 11:6). Finally, it was this Spirit who equipped people with skill and strength for creative work (Exod. 31:1-11; cf. 1 Kings 7:14; Hag. 2:5; Zech. 4:6).

In short, the Spirit of God in the Old Testament is God active as creator, controller, revealer, quickener, and enabler. He made himself present to people in order that they might know him and his will and live with each other in accordance with it. Always the reference is to God himself, who is present and at work; the reference is never merely to blind power or depersonalized force.

The Holy Spirit in the New Testament

In the New Testament all that the Old Testament says about God's Spirit is taken for granted, and the Holy Spirit at Pentecost is identified explicitly with the Old Testament Spirit of God (Acts 2:16-21; 4:25; 28:25; Heb. 3:7-11; 10:15; 1 Pet. 1:11; 2 Pet. 1:19-21). The Spirit's personhood, however, is evident in the verbs of personal action—hear, speak, witness, convince, show, lead, guide, teach, command, forbid, desire, give speech, help, intercede with groans—that are used to tell us what he does (John 14:26; 15:26; 16:7-15; Acts 2:4; 8:29; 13:2; 16:6-7; 21:11; Rom. 8:14, 16, 26-27; Gal. 4:6; 5:17, 18; Heb. 3:7; 10:15; 1 Pet. 1:11; Rev. 2:7, 11, 17, 29, etc.). It is evident also from the fact that he can be lied to and grieved (Acts 5:3; Eph. 4:30; cf. Isa. 63:10). It appears with supreme clarity when Jesus in John's gospel introduces the Spirit as the Paraclete (14:16, 25; 15:26; 16:7), for this rich word—which means by turns Counselor, Helper, Strengthener, Supporter, Adviser, Advocate, and Ally—signifies a role that only a personal agent could fulfill. Jesus confirms this by calling the Spirit "another" Paraclete, who will continue his ministry after his departure (14:16); this is a way of informing us that the Spirit is a person as truly as Jesus himself is. John seems to strengthen the point by using the personal pronoun *ekeinos* ("he") to render Jesus' references to the Spirit, when Greek grammar more naturally would have used the neuter *ekeino* ("it") to agree with the neuter noun *pneuma* ("Spirit," the Greek equivalent of *ruach*). This personal pronoun—which appears in John 14:26; 15:26; and 16:8, 13-14—is the more striking because in 14:17, where the Spirit is first introduced, John uses the grammatically appropriate neuter pronouns (*ho* and *auto*). The subsequent shift to the masculine undergirds his theology and was given under the Spirit's own inspiration.

However, to understand what is said about the Spirit and the Son tritheistically would be a mistake. No apostolic writer thinks of the Father, the Son, and the Spirit as independent deities. In the New Testament, the distinct personhood of the Spirit, along with that of the Son, is only ever thought or spoken of as part of the revealed reality of the one God of Israel. Decisive for this way of thinking was the recognition of the risen, ascended, and enthroned Jesus as a person to be worshiped and prayed to alongside, yet in distinction from, the one whom he called Father, so that it was right to say to Jesus what Thomas said to him—"My Lord and my God!" (John 20:28)—just as it was and is right to address those words to the Father. And from this recognition of Jesus' divinity the apostolic writers go on to link the Holy Spirit with him in what is effectively a parity relationship, one that combines solidarity in redemptive action with coequal divine dignity. This is in direct line with Jesus' declaration that the Holy Spirit in his post-Pentecostal ministry, specifically in his work as the Spirit of Christ, would be the second Paraclete, replacing Jesus permanently in order to mediate constantly to Christians the presence—not physical, but yet real and beneficent—of both the Son and the Father (John 14:16-23).

Many New Testament passages speak of the Son and the Spirit side by side, correlating and coordinating them in a way that is clearly deliberate: see, for instance, Acts 9:31 (divine communion); Romans 8:9-11 (divine indwelling); Romans 8:27, 34 (divine intercession); Romans 15:30 (Christian motivation; cf. Phil. 2:1); 1 Corinthians 6:11 (justification); Hebrews 10:29 (apostasy); and Revelation 2:1, 7-8, 11 (divine revelation). More striking still are the triadic passages linking Father, Son, and Spirit as collaborators in a single plan of grace (see, for example, John 14:16–16:15; Rom. 8; 1 Cor. 12:4-6; 2 Cor. 13:14; Eph. 1:3-13; 2:18; 3:14-19; 4:4-6; 2 Thess. 2:13-14; 1 Pet. 1:2). These testimonies show that as in terms of role the Spirit acts as agent—colleague, we might say—of the Father and the Son, so in terms of deity he is on a par with them, and in our doxology he should be honored with them and praised.

Nor is this all. Though the Spirit is nowhere explicitly called God, the New Testament writers intimate his deity in ways clearer than any yet mentioned. Thus, "holy," like "Lord," is an Old Testament designation of God, "the Holy One"; and as the New Testament writers repeatedly use "Lord" to refer to Jesus, so they call the Spirit "holy" no less than eighty-nine times. Again, "glory" in the Old Testament means deity in manifestation, Yahweh being "the God of glory" (Ps. 29:3); and in the New Testament, as the Father is "the glorious Father" (Eph. 1:17) and Jesus is "the Lord of glory" (1 Cor. 2:8; James 2:1), so the Spirit is "the Spirit of glory" (1 Pet. 4:14). Similarly, as the Father and the Son give "life" (a relationship of conscious response to God's grace in love, peace, and joy), so the Spirit gives "life" (see John 5:21, 26; 6:32-33, 63; Rom. 8:2; 2 Cor. 3:6). All three persons are thus identified with Yahweh in the Old Testament, the Spirit as directly as the two others.

And there is more. Lying to the Holy Spirit is diagnosed as lying "not . . . to men but to God" (Acts 5:3-4). Also, Jesus declares that the name of God, into which his disciples are to be baptized, is a tripersonal name: "the name of the Father and of the Son and of the Holy Spirit" (Matt. 28:19). "The name" means the designated party. "Name" is singular here, for there is only one God, but God's "name"—his "Christian name," as Barth called it—is tripersonal. Furthermore, John starts his letters to the churches by wishing them grace and peace "from him who is, and who was, and who is to come, and from the seven spirits before his throne, and from Jesus Christ" (Rev. 1:4-5). The "seven spirits," according to the numerical symbolism of the book, signify the Holy Spirit in the perfection of his power, and when the Spirit is set between the Father and the Son as the second of the three personal sources of divine blessing, no room remains for doubt as to his coequal deity.

Whether one finds a doctrine of the Trinity in the New Testament depends on what one means by "doctrine." If it is proper to give the name "doctrine" to a position that is explicit and defined, it cannot be improper to give the same name to that which is basic and presuppositional to what is defined. The Trinitarian way of thinking about God is in fact basic and presuppositional to all the New Testament's explicit soteriology because it is the answer to the problem with the unity of God raised by the fact of Christ, the event of Pentecost, and the shape of subsequent Christian experience. It is therefore pertinent and necessary to affirm that the New Testament writers teach the doctrine of the Trinity. It is injurious to their teaching to deny it, as is fashionable today. Though innocent of later Trinitarian formulations, these writers do in fact think of God in the tripersonal way that the later formulations were devised to safeguard, and they reject other conceptions as anti-Christian (cf. 1 Tim. 3:16–4:5; 2 Tim. 3:1-9; 2 Pet. 2:1; 1 John 2:18-27; 4:1-6). The true path is to affirm this, and thereby negate all forms, old and new, of the idea that the Spirit is a creature of, a function of, or merely a title for a unipersonal God. No version of this unitarian idea can express accurately or adequately what the New Testament writers mean when they speak of the Spirit.

The statement that post-Pentecostal Christian experience raised a problem with the unity of God no doubt requires explanation. The problem was posed by the fact that post-Pentecostal experience, the experience of being "in the Spirit" and "in the Lord," involved awareness of a dual relationship—to God as Father and to Jesus as Savior and Master—that was seen as dependent on the personally indwelling Holy Spirit (Rom. 8:9). This awareness prompted the question about whether God is tripersonal, a question that undoubtedly presupposed some instruction (and the Gospels show clearly who the first instructor was). Thus it is hard to doubt that experience within the threefold relationship shaped some of the New Testament expositions of it, Paul's in particular, and so became a means of establishing the way of thinking about God that underlies it.

Here it is appropriate to characterize the New Testament sense of God with some exactness. It is uniformly Trinitarian; more particularly, it is Christ-centered and, in its own view of itself, Spirit-generated to the core. It is true to say that the Christian awareness is of God above, beside, and within, but that does not adequately express the New Testament view; we need to be more precise. The authentic Christian awareness of God, as the New Testament writers exhibit it, produced three foundational convictions. First, it generated the sense that God in heaven, this world's maker and judge, is our Father, who sent his Son to redeem us; who adopted us into his family; who loves us, watches over us, listens to us, cares for us, and showers gifts upon us; who preserves us for the inheritance of glory that he keeps in store for us; and to whom we have access through Christ, by the Spirit (Matt. 6:1-18, 24-33; Luke 11:1-13; John 14:21; 16:27; 20:17; Rom. 8:15-17; Gal. 4:4-7; Eph. 2:18). Second, it produced the assurance that Jesus Christ, who is now personally in heaven, nonetheless makes himself present to us by the Spirit to stand by us, to love, lead, assure, quicken, uphold, and encourage us, and to use us in his work as in weakness we trust him (Matt. 28:20; John 15:1-8; Rom. 15:18; 1 Cor. 6:17; 15:45; 2 Cor. 12:9; Eph. 3:14-19; 2 Tim. 4:17). Third, it produced the recognition that the Holy Spirit dwells in us for several reasons: (1) to sustain in us what nowadays is called a personal and existential understanding of gospel truth (1 Cor. 2:14-16; 12:3; 1 John 2:20-27; 5:7-8, 20); (2) to maintain in our consciousness our fellowship with the Father and the Son, and to assure us that this love relationship is permanent and that glorification lies at the end of it (John 14:18-23; Rom. 8:14-25; Gal. 4:4-7; 1 John 1:3; 3:1-2, 24); (3) to reshape us in ethical correspondence to Christ (2 Cor. 3:18; Gal. 5:22-24; Eph. 5:1-2) as he induces us to accept suffering with Christ, which is the road to final glory (Rom. 8:12-17; 2 Cor. 1:5; 4:7–5:5; Phil. 3:7-10, 20-21); (4) to equip us with abilities for loving, personal worship of God in praise and prayer (John 4:23-24; 1 Cor. 13:1; 14:2, 26-32; Eph. 6:18; Phil. 3:1; Jude 20) and for loving, personal ministry to others about Christ (Rom. 12:4-21; 1 Cor.

12:4-13; 1 Pet. 4:10-11); (5) to engender realization of our present moral weakness and inadequacy of achievement (Rom. 7:14-25; 8:22-27; Gal. 5:16-17), and to make us long for the future life of bodily resurrection and renewal, the Spirit's present ministry to us being the firstfruits (Rom. 8:23) and the initial installment of that life and guaranteeing the rest (2 Cor. 1:22; 5:5; Eph. 1:14).

This structured, tripersonal sense of God is what constitutes New Testament Christianity. The central constituent of this sense of God is the awareness that "the Spirit of your Father" (Matt. 10:20) in his role as "the Spirit of [God's] Son" and "the Spirit of sonship," "the Spirit of grace," "the Spirit of truth," and "the Spirit of wisdom" (Gal. 4:6; Acts 16:7; Rom. 8:2, 9, 15; Heb. 10:29; John 14:17; Acts 6:3, 10) is now given to abide with all Christians. The New Testament witness is that as believers know God in and through Jesus Christ, so they know Jesus Christ in and through the Holy Spirit. This makes Christian experience—that is, the Christian's affective awareness of the divine—radically different from its Jewish and Gentile counterparts.

It seems clear that the apostles' convictions and formulations concerning the Spirit are the product, the intellectual precipitate, of living in the Spirit and directly experiencing Christ in the manner described, though passion for abstract orthodoxy has sometimes betrayed evangelicals into overlooking this fact. That the apostles' convictions are divinely revealed truths, and as such are matters of doctrine and norms of faith, is a fixed point, but that does not necessarily mean that these convictions appeared in apostolic minds ready-made. It is more natural to suppose that they crystallized out of the experiential-ethical transformation that those who received the Spirit, the apostles among them, underwent. The insights of the New Testament writers concerning the Spirit arose, no doubt, from the words of Jesus, but were distilled into their later and fuller form via response to experienced deity under the sovereign leading of the Spirit. The idea that because apostolic teaching is revealed truth it must have come to the apostles by some means other than noting, describing, and reflecting upon their own experience of God seems groundless. The apostles' evident view is that experience of the Spirit comes spontaneously and directly but reveals its authenticity by creating an immediate awareness of the presence of the Christ of the gospel in love and power, and by evoking a heartfelt response of confession, celebration, repentance, obedience, and praise. Those who share this experience, the apostles assume, will know that they have received the Spirit (cf. Acts 2:13-21; Rom. 8:23, 26-27; Gal. 3:2; Eph. 1:14; 1 John 3:24; 4:13; Rev.

1:10). The apostles recognized that some who claimed to be experiencing the life of the Spirit had to be challenged, for major error concerning Christ's person, place, authority, and law would show those claims to be false (see 1 Cor. 12:3; 14:37-38; 1 John 3:24– 4:13), and what looked like such error was sometimes found among the supposedly Spirit-led. But the essential clarity of the Spirit's action in Christ's professed disciples is taken for granted throughout the New Testament. The apostles did not think it difficult to judge when the Spirit was at work, nor did they doubt their own participation in the Spirit's ministry. So there is no reason to doubt, and every reason to suppose, that their theology of the Spirit reached its full form in and through this participation, rather than being given in revelatory experiences distinct from it.

The New Testament understanding of the Holy Spirit is, of course, given its fullest expression in Paul, who ranges wider, analyzes more deeply, and reasons more tautly than any other apostle. Were we to attempt to draw out all the implications of the profound statements in his letters (Rom. 7–8; 14:17; 15:17-21; 1 Cor. 2; 3:16-17; 6:9-20; 12–14; 2 Cor. 3; Gal. 3:14; 4:6; 4:21–6:10; Eph. 1:13-20; 2:18-22; 3:14-19; 4:1-16, 30; 5:15-33; 6:10-20; 1 Thess. 1:2-10; 5:16-20; 2 Tim. 1:6-14; Titus 3:3-7), we would be composing a book on this subject alone rather than ending a brief section of a chapter. But the outlines of Paul's thought about the Spirit, as distinct from the wealth and depth of that thought, can be stated in a brief and simple way.

Salvation through Christ—Christ crucified, risen, enthroned, reigning, and coming again; Christ known, loved, and adored as our path and our prize, our deliverer and our destiny—is Paul's constant theme. Salvation is the life of the new and eternal order, the life of heaven begun for us on earth through the coming of Christ and his Spirit. For Paul, the expected messianic "age to come" has arrived. For a period of time, "this age" and the "age to come" are coextensive with one another and in Christian life are experienced together. Yet these two ages, these two realms of existence, though presently in proximity to one another, are as different as light is from darkness. In Christ the new has arrived, and through him the old is passing away, soon to be eclipsed by God's judgment and cosmic renovation. Just as "flesh," as Paul uses it, is always some aspect of life under the old order, so "spirit"—always when used of God's Spirit and almost always when used of the human spirit, the self to which the divine Spirit ministers—points to the life of the new order. When Paul speaks of the God-sent Holy Spirit, his perspective is always eschatological, looking forward to the end, of which our present experience of redemption and life in the Spirit is the beginning. The Spirit is the gift of the new age, the guarantee and foretaste, the pledge and first installment of what is to come when the fullness of salvation is revealed at Christ's return (Eph. 1:13-14; Rom. 8:23). It is this teaching on the relation between the old and the new, the flesh and the Spirit, the historical and the eschatological that forms the whole context within which Paul expounds his doctrines of the church and of salvation. It is in this context that he elaborates on his doctrine of the Spirit.

We will always misunderstand the work of the Spirit if we misunderstand his person, for he can do what he does only because of who he is. The Holy Spirit can inspire our Scriptures, miraculously create the humanity of Jesus, raise him from the dead, recreate human life, and fill and fashion the church to be Christ's instrument because he is God. He can lead, teach, instruct, and pray because he is personal. He is our eternal contemporary, present with us in every moment of our lives, the one because of whom we have savingly believed on Christ and without whom we could not live in this present age confident of Christ's victory.

The Holy Spirit in the Early Centuries

It might be tempting to think that as we move from the New Testament period to the centuries that immediately followed it, we are moving from one world to another. That, at least, is the appearance. The spontaneous exercise of spiritual gifts rapidly gave way to organized ministry. The participation of the whole congregation in worship was quickly replaced by a fixed liturgy and its near total monopolization by the clergy. The association of New Testament churches, formerly held together by apostolic authority, now increasingly was bonded by ecclesiastical power. The exercise of the Spirit's gifts, especially of signs and wonders, diminished, and as the church readied itself for its conflict with the Roman state as well as with the growing excesses of heresy, it assumed a form markedly different from what it had had in the New Testament.

This might lead us to think that beneath the changing circumstances was a changing understanding of the Holy Spirit. But that cannot be deduced from the evidence. In actual fact, the Holy Spirit appears to have been widely experienced in patristic times. The terse and compact phrases of the creeds, especially those of Nicea and Constantinople, point back to this, for each and every word refers to a fundamental experience in the life of believers. To say this in no way contradicts the equally true assertion that for the fathers each and every word of the creeds had to be based upon Scripture as they understood it. The patristic church was deliberately and self-consciously biblical in its understanding. The early fathers even preferred the wording of their creeds to be biblical, which was why they felt so uneasy with the term *homoousios* (of the same substance) in the Nicene Creed. Thus the creedal articles we will consider should be seen to have arisen out of the nexus between experience, biblical exegesis, and theological reflection in which the biblical Word was always authoritative but never disassociated from experience on the one side and reflection on the other.

But why, you may ask, is this historical sketch traveling only as far as the patristic period? Have there not been significant developments since then? Are the creeds—and here we are considering particularly the Constantinopolitan Creed—in some way sacrosanct?

The answers to these questions are simple. Every age has posed particular challenges to the truth of God's Word because each age has brought to it particular questions. These questions arise out of the matrix of social, political, cultural, and psychological factors that make up what the Bible calls "the world" in each age. Thus it is possible to identify in the church's past the ages in which particular doctrines have received concentrated attention and, as a result, have usually reached a high level of refinement. This is what James Orr sought to recognize in his *Progress of Dogma,* and what Karl Barth assumed in his *Church Dogmatics.* And it is not difficult to see that the early centuries produced substantial debate over the Godhead, debate that gave rise to classic formulations. These formulations are not infallible; they are not revelatory. They do, however, prescribe what has become the historic Christian position down through the centuries. For that reason they need to be considered briefly here.

Although the doctrine of the Trinity can be found—albeit only in rudimentary form sometimes—in the earliest Christian writers, the questions raised about the divinity of the Son by Arius and his followers in the early fourth century struck the church with great force. Arius's argument was not itself particularly forceful, but the church's thought on this point had not yet jelled into conviction. Even though the Nicene Creed affirmed that Son and Father were "of the same substance," that the Son was not in any sense a creature, it took the church as a whole about sixty years before it embraced this affirmation as its own settled conviction.

From the doctrine of the Son, the church then moved to the doctrine of the Spirit. In the year A.D. 380, Gregory of Nazianzus declared that the subject of the Holy Spirit presented special difficulties because those who had defended the Son's divinity had become worn out by the barrage of questions and had no appetite for further debate along those lines. He went on to note, however, that current proposals on the Spirit—that he was a creature, or merely a force, or a person whose divinity was less than that of Father and Son—called into question the Christian understanding of the Godhead. In response, Gregory of Nazianzus, his younger brother Gregory of Nyssa, and Basil made it their special business to do for the doctrine of the Spirit what Athanasius had done for the doctrine of the Son. Indeed, they not only followed Athanasius but also built upon and enlarged his understanding of the Spirit's full divinity. The importance of this definitional work and the presence of a growing conviction about the Holy Spirit are clearly seen when the single article on the Spirit from the Nicene Creed (A.D. 325) is compared with its expanded form in the Constantinopolitan Creed (A.D. 381). The Nicene Creed simply affirms belief "in the Holy Spirit." The Constantinopolitan Creed expands this affirmation of belief thus: "And in the Holy Spirit, the Lord and life-giver, Who proceeds from the Father, Who with the Father and the Son is together worshipped and together glorified, Who spoke through the prophets; in one holy Catholic and apostolic Church. We confess one baptism for the remission of sins; we look forward to the resurrection of the dead and the life of the world to come. Amen."

However, Basil's treatise, *De Spiritu Sancto* (A.D. 375), moved hesitantly toward the Athanasian doctrine of the consubstantiality of the Spirit with the Father. Basil privately admitted to not wanting to call the Spirit "God," and he went on to say that by avoiding this provocative statement he would win over his opponents. But his opponents, the Macedonians, were in no mood for compromise, and so Basil moved slowly from denying that the Spirit was a creature to affirming his full divinity. His doctrine, however, was stated more indirectly than directly. Indeed, the treatise itself was occasioned by complaints about his liturgical habit of giving praise to the Holy Spirit "with the Father and Son."

Thus the assertion of the Spirit's divinity could be made in ways other than a theoretical defense of his *homoousion* or consubstantiality with the Father, for the Spirit's essential divinity was also revealed in what he did. If the Spirit was the life-giver and sanctifier, he was doing the work not of a creature but of the Creator. The Constantinopolitan Creed, therefore, asserted the Spirit's divinity not in the difficult language of *homoousios* used of the Son in Nicea but in Basil's more indirect way: "Who with the Father and the Son is together worshipped and together glorified." And the equally controversial phrase "from the substance of the Father" that the Nicene Creed used of the Son was carefully reworded in a biblical phrase: "Who proceeds from the Father." It is an almost verbatim quotation from John 15:26. The Macedonians, who were contesting the Spirit's divinity as the Arians had the Son's, saw the point and refused to comply with the creed. Their perception of the creed's teaching was correct. The doctrine of the Trinity affirmed by the creed implied the deity of the Spirit, and the formulation of the Spirit's procession undergirded it.

With Augustine, attention was once more focused not on the person of the Holy Spirit per se but on the doctrine of the Trinity within which the Spirit must be understood. However, Augustine shifted from thinking of the Trinity in almost mathematical terms to doing so in psychological images. If the human being is in the image of God and if there is a threefold structure to the human soul, then we have at hand ways of thinking of the triunity that are comprehensible. Thus we might picture God as the lover, as the loved, and as love. The Holy Spirit is the chain or bond of love linking the Father and the Son. The Holy Spirit, Augustine said, is "a certain ineffable communion of Father and Son, which may well be called affection but is more fittingly called love." He also went on to assert that the Spirit proceeds from both the Father and the Son. The immediate effect of this, of course, was to secure for the Son full co-equality with the Father inasmuch as the Spirit proceeds from him as well as from the Father. But Augustine intended more. However flawed the analogies were, however mistaken the conceptuality might be, he also wanted in these ways to declare the Spirit's full deity and his complete personality.

By the time of Augustine, then, the conclusion could safely be drawn that the Holy Spirit could not be less personal than the personal beings he has made, for they are the mirror in which the Trinity is reflected. Nor could the Spirit be less than fully divine if he does the work that only God himself can do. The evidence for these conclusions came, of course, from a consideration not only of who the Spirit is but also of what he does. What he does, therefore, illumines who he is, and who he is explains what he does. This aspect of patristic thinking on the Holy Spirit will be discussed more fully in Chapter II.

Conclusion

The doctrine of God's triunity is the only way we can do justice to the biblical teaching. God is not comprehensible except as the one God—Father, Son and Holy Spirit—for that is what he is and that is how he has disclosed himself to us. The early fathers came to this realization slowly and painfully, but their conclusions were right and have subsequently borne the tests of time.

It is true that in some Third World churches there is an inadequate appreciation of this early Christian history, even as, for different reasons, there is sometimes a reaction in Western churches to old creedal formularies on the Trinity. In the one case they seem irrelevant and in the other anachronistic.

It is this historic understanding of the Godhead, however, that needs to be recovered with renewed freshness in our own time. Without a full Trinitarian understanding, Christian faith offers no viable alternative to other monotheistic faiths such as Islam. More than that, it is easily reduced to simply one component to be included in a new and higher religious synthesis. Alternatively, if the person and the work of the Spirit are obscured, misunderstood, or denied, the door is often opened to sub-Christian cults, examples of which are found in many places in Africa. The result of all of these aberrations is that Christian faith is supposedly maintained but Christ is usually bypassed. And that should come as no surprise to us, because it is the work of the Holy Spirit to glorify him.

In the Western, secularized societies where so many people struggle with anonymity and meaninglessness, the reality of the Holy Spirit is indispensable to the presentation of Christian faith. He, the eternal, distinct, equal third member of the Godhead, is also *personal*. He hears us, grieves over us, convicts us, humbles us, exhorts us, and prays over us. He illumines our minds, regenerates our hearts, bends our wills, applies the benefits of Christ's death to us, transforms us, fills us, empowers us, and leads us to love and worship Christ, by whom alone we are saved. He can do all of these things because he is personal, and it is his work to keep our relationship to the Father and the Son central in our consciousness. That this can happen is glorious news to men and women lost in societies where individuals are not much valued and where human worth itself is in question.

In this connection it is important to remember that the typical preaching in Acts offered both forgiveness and the Holy Spirit. The coming of the Spirit, either in promise or in fact, is included in the record of seven evangelistic sermons (2:33, 39; 3:19; 5:31-32; 8:15ff.; 9:17; 10:43-44, 47; 19:6). Only in one instance is forgiveness offered without mention of the Holy Spirit (13:38-39), although in the truncated accounts of four other occasions salvation is discussed without mention of either forgiveness or the Spirit (4:8; 14:8ff.; 16:31; 17:22). Thus the gospel that was offered and that we need to declare with fresh power is one in which right standing with God is held out through Christ and the indwelling Spirit is there for those who believe on him.

Nevertheless, the church has frequently lost sight of the Holy Spirit and has at times grievously misunderstood him and his work. It may seem remarkable, for example, that the early fathers, whose minds were filled with the same Scriptures as are ours, were so slow to arrive at clear convictions about the person of the Holy Spirit. Why were they so hesitant to say what seems to us so obvious?

Or is it so obvious? If it is, then why is belief in a full-orbed doctrine of the Trinity such a rarity in theological circles today? And why are so many casual alliances struck between the work of the Spirit and socio-political movements and developments in non-Christian religions?

Rather than shaking our heads over the snail's pace in patristic thinking on the Spirit, we would be wiser to acknowledge our own fallibility and obtuseness, our own propensity to fashion God in our own image and to build intellectual idols pleasing to our own twentieth-century tastes. Biblical orthodoxy will always be vulnerable to the inroads of heresy until Christ returns; it will always be a focal point in the conflict between Christ and Satan, the Spirit and the flesh. There is no better way to begin a study on the Holy Spirit, therefore, than to confess our own sinfulness and our corresponding need for his guidance and illumination. May we do so now!

Chapter II

The World and Its Religions

There are moments when the divine attributes of omniscience and omnipresence seem almost within our grasp. Certainly it is the case that the advent of television has given us a window on the world, and the "information industry" has provided us with an understanding of the world that is unprecedented. Furthermore, the modern "miracle" of jet travel has effectively shrunk our globe. Time and space are not the obstacles they used to be. We can participate, albeit vicariously, in all of the events that are shaping and shaking our globe; we can acquire information on most subjects with astonishing rapidity; and we can be anywhere we want, even across oceans, in a matter of hours.

The full impact of all of this upon the human psyche is not easy to gauge. Omniscience and omnipresence do not rest comfortably within our mortal, fallible, and limited constitutions. It may be that the drug culture is in part an attempt to flee from the disconcerting realities with which our "godlike" capabilities confront us. But escape, however it is sought, is not an option for Christians. We therefore need to come to terms with the world not as it used to be or as we would like it to be, but as it is. In order to do this, we will begin by considering the Holy Spirit's role in creation and revelation; next we will consider the fact and meaning of non-Christian religions in our world; and finally we will define for ourselves what our role ought to be in these contexts.

The Spirit in Creation

It is one of the curious ironies of our time that in the West so much of life is depersonalized while in many of the underdeveloped nations so much of nature is personalized. Affluent, educated Westerners do not see God or the supernatural behind or within the physical world, whereas many in

Third World countries not only fear the spirits who inhabit nature but often personalize its blind forces. The truth is found at neither one extreme nor the other. But it is nevertheless also ironic that the Western academic machinery has produced a perception of the world that is really so thoroughly ignorant. It is in several ways more uninformed and more aberrant than the "superstitious" outlook of the underdeveloped nations that it is so quick to deride.

And perhaps the largest irony of all is found in the fact that the modern Western view of nature would not have been possible without Christian faith. Today, science and technology are parasites that live off the Christian worldview. Neither can exist unless there is an objective world, a world that exists apart from the perception of the viewer, and neither can function unless there is a world that operates uniformly and predictably. In much Eastern philosophy, neither of these requirements is present: the world is considered neither objective nor predictable. It is perhaps not surprising that, as a result, science and technology were born and have largely flourished in the West. It is here that Christian assumptions provide the needed underpinnings. The world is objective because God has brought it into existence, and it is predictable because his control of it is stable. Furthermore, his relationship to creation is what also gives the world its moral framework. These ideas deserve exploration.

It is, of course, as the divine *ruach,* the loosed power of God and the bearer of life, that we first encounter the Spirit. His creative presence is vividly expressed in the image of his "brooding" above the unordered chaos on the morning of creation (Gen. 1:1-2). The language of creation in Scripture encompasses the first act of bringing something out of nothing (Gen. 2:4; Ps. 90:2; Acts 17:24; Col. 1:16; Rev. 4:11), the subsequent ordering and superintendence of the created process (Gen. 1:7, 16, 19, 26; Ps. 89:47; 104:26; Isa. 45:7, 12; Amos 4:13), and the ongoing, providential sustaining of the whole created order (Deut. 32:18; Ps. 74:17; 104:30; Isa. 43:1, 7, 21; 45:7; Acts 17:26). Because the creation is made *ex nihilo* (Heb. 11:3), it is both different and separate from God. The account of creation in Genesis 1 stands in contrast to the creation myths of the surrounding cultures, and we are left in no doubt that the natural human tendency to see God in everything and everything in God is disallowed by Genesis. At the same time, through his Spirit, God is immanent in creation, sustaining and guiding it. The equally natural and mistaken human tendency to think that God is aloof and withdrawn from his creation is therefore contradicted. He is both distinct from and yet related to the created order. He is both above and within it.

It is this relationship that has imparted to the creation meaning that goes beyond the mere brute facts of its working. For God has disclosed within it inklings of his presence and glimmerings of his morality so that it is not possible to see nature as nothing but a theater of the absurd. Rather, it is the theater of the divine. In its structure, orderliness, beauty, and design, it points beyond itself to its holy creator. In the "rains and fruitful seasons," in "food and gladness" we are to see a divine witness (Acts 14:16-17, RSV; cf. Ps. 19:1-2). And in the shape he has given to human civilizations, he has provided the grounds for men and women to "reach out for him and find him." Within human life there is sufficient intimation of the spiritual and moral reality of God that we should not confuse him with inanimate images of gold or silver or stone (Acts 17:24-29).

This dim perception of God, this twilight knowledge, is heightened internally by the presence of human conscience. Life reveals that it is more than matter, and conscience reveals that it is more than life. The human being ever stands in the moral presence of God, from which there can be no escape and before which there is a relentless summons to accountability. The heavens themselves reveal God's moral nature and his wrath (Rom. 1:19-20), and human conscience resonates with this disclosure, leaving us without excuse for failing to honor God and for indulging in moral and religious perversion (Rom. 1:21, 25, 32; 2:1-4, 12-16).

Thus, through the Spirit's work in creation, a disclosure of God's moral existence is made. It is a disclosure of law but not of the gospel, for what it reveals is that sinning precipitates the wrath of God but not that our sin can provide the occasion of God's forgiveness through Christ. It is, therefore, a revelation addressed to humans as humans: it tells them no more than they would have known were they not fallen. It is not a revelation addressed to them as sinners, telling them what they need to know to be redeemed from their sin.

Non-Christian Religions

We are now in a position to see clearly why it is that ours is a world that is both incurably religious and persistently aberrant, for we are all, at all times, both the image bearers of God and rebels against that God. This paradox is worth pondering further.

The religious dimension of life is evident throughout our world, although it is well-disguised in the secular West. Yet it is not difficult even here to detect among secular humanists, as well as atheistic Marxists, characteristics that are remarkable for their religious nature. The search for peace and harmony, the personal quest of many in the West, is essentially a religious quest. Peace and harmony used to be sought through external gods and goddesses; now they are pursued through the internal "gods" and "goddesses" of private experience. The pursuit of power is also a religious quest, whether it is sought in the world of spirits or, as in the case of Marxists, in the control of human spirits. For it is in that control, they believe, that evil will be eliminated and something not unlike a millennium will finally result.

These and other expressions of religious interest testify to the inescapable but perverted presence of general revelation, perhaps, most importantly, in its moral dimension, for even the Gentiles "show that the requirements of the law are written on their hearts, their consciences also bearing witness, and their thoughts now accusing, now even defending them" (Rom. 2:15). All religions develop myths and rituals to cope with this factor in human experience. It cannot be ignored. But conscience, uninstructed by the Word of God, may not always function correctly, and certainly it is the case that it is often masked by cultural and ideological factors.

In theistic religions such as Judaism, Christianity, and Islam as well as in traditional spirit religions, a bad conscience usually expresses itself in a sense of guilt and a corresponding need for forgiveness. Nontheistic religions, however, give little place to guilt. They are shame-oriented. This is particularly true of philosophical Hinduism, Theravada Buddhism, Confucianism, and Shintoism. Shame is the feeling of self-exposure before others—be it from ignorance or lawbreaking—or the loss of face and of self-esteem. Thus, coping with shame is fundamental to interpersonal relationships in most Asian cultures, and provides striking evidence of natural revelation filtered through a cultural context. Likewise, among the Bantu in Africa, shame rather than guilt is key to social life. Shame, however, is understood not only individually but also collectively. Sin is breaking the obligation of the community. Family, clan, or tribe is invariably involved.

If guilt and shame testify to our moral-religious capacity, idolatry is one of the evidences of the perversion of that capacity. The key to understanding it is given to us in Romans 1:18-23, where Paul affirms that there is truth about God in all human experience but that this truth is deliberately suppressed. It is because we are rebels that we fashion gods in the place of the one, true God, and as we become captive to the gods of our creation, God abandons us to the consequences of our own depravity.

Idolatry, then, is the worship of self-made images, be they material or spiritual ones, as substitutes for the living God. The purpose in idolatry is always the same. It is to displace God, to replace him by gods of our own liking and, insofar as they are substitutes, to control them. We thus seek to become God through our gods. To be sure, idolatry does not always express itself so blatantly. In some religions images are used with the intent, it is said, of inspiring faith and leading us to true worship. It is on this basis that Hindus, for example, defend the use of phallic symbols, the sacred bull of Saivism, and the half-elephant, half-man of Ganesh. Such images are designed to personify divine attributes and to lead worshipers toward self-realization. Much the same can be said about the images of Buddha and of the Virgin Mary. But however its nature is concealed and however idolatry actually functions, the result is always the same: the reality, character, and power of God are challenged, and the human spirit slips into the terrible bondage it has wrought for itself in its challenge.

It is important to understand that idolatry is expressed in forms that are not only material but also mental. Yoga, for example, is a subtle form of idolatry. It is a method widely used in Hindu and Buddhist religions to achieve ultimate spiritual release. Its growing popularity with Western youth indicates that a radical shift is taking place in their concept of spirituality. In the early stages or steps, yoga is a well-developed technique for release from stress and for the conservation of bodily and psychic energy. But in its progressive and final steps, yoga is designed to produce a radical change in the mode of human consciousness. The goal is pure self-consciousness, absorption into Ultimate Reality, or the realization of final Nirvana. *Samadhi,* the trance of pure bliss, is the ultimate religious experience of Vedanta yoga. It is the end of all personhood and moral consciousness.

In the affluent West, the most prevalent forms of idolatry are different and overtly nonreligious: covetousness, greed, and sexual sin. (Paul links these sins to idolatry in Rom. 1:21-32; 1 Cor. 5:11; Gal. 5:19; Eph. 5:5; and Col. 3:5.) The experience of affluence undoubtedly creates both an appetite for possessions and a worldview in which the meaning of life is decided in terms of what can be bought, owned, sold, and used. To have is to be. This is not only the seedbed in which greed and covetousness take root, but also the seedbed that produces the rapacious alternatives to the truth, worship, and service of God.

What can be said about affluence applies with equal force to our current fascination with and exploitation of sexuality. Carnality in all of its forms—from *Playboy* to the debauchery of pornographic movies— offers liberation of the spirit through sexual experience. What it actually produces is only bondage, a bondage that is addictive. No matter how demeaned and debauched the sexuality may be, it demands of its devotees their total allegiance. It becomes a way of life that is a substitute for that way which the Law and Word of God hold out. It is idolatry. And it participates in the judgment that God pronounces on all other forms of idolatry.

Because they are idolatrous, non-Christian religions as well as materialistic philosophies (such as Marxism) and materialistic orientations (such as the affluence of the West) do not represent paths to God. None are partial expressions of Christian truth. Yet the cultural pressures in many countries have forced Christians to reconsider the exclusive claims of Christ, especially in terms of the non-Christian religions. This reconsideration has been given theological expression.

In the nineteenth century, Protestant Liberalism spawned a "history of religions" school that in the end sought not merely to chronicle the life of religion but to synthesize its various expressions. The presupposition of this quest was that the divine is to be found by, with, and under all human personality. The divine Spirit and the human spirit were thus merged into one another, the latter being the vehicle of expression of the former. Religion in its formal expressions, therefore, aimed at identifying, clarifying, and nurturing the divine in human life. On the Roman Catholic side, the Modernists argued the same point.

Protestant Liberalism was destroyed by the double onslaught of social catastrophe (the Second World War in Europe and the Great Depression in North America) and neo-orthodoxy. The theological change was led primarily by Karl Barth, who chastised the Liberals for making God after their own experiential image. God had become a Protestant Liberal nine feet tall, Barth claimed. And in 1907, the experimentation with ideas such as these came to an abrupt halt in Catholic circles with the publication of the encyclical *Pascendi Gregis*. This was followed by a period of severe housecleaning and discipline, culminating in 1910 in the institution of the Oath against Modernism, to which all Catholic priests would swear.

But human memory is short. By the 1960s the old Liberal ideas were once again being canvased, mainly in World Council of Churches circles. On the Catholic side, the Second Vatican Council took the essence of the Modernist interest in non-Christian religions and gave it formal approval. The Council argued that God's grace, a grace sufficient for eternal salvation, is given not only to those in non-Christian religions but even to some atheists. By this grace, atheists who are without blame for their atheism can find the help they need to live a good life, as a result of which they can be saved. Thus it was argued that men and women may declare themselves to be atheists on a cognitive level, yet may still be the recipients of grace at the level of being.

The Council did not use or make reference to Karl Rahner's notion of the "anonymous Christian," but the thought is plainly there. And many commentators on the documents, especially the opening chapters of the "Constitution on the Church," have pondered where the boundaries lie in describing "the people of God." Who are these people? Clearly they include Christians other than Catholics. But are members of non-Christian faiths included? Is it possible, perhaps, to argue that "the people of God" is co-extensive with humanity? This kind of consideration has led naturally into a discussion about "the cosmic Christ." If God's people include members of other faiths, then it follows that Christ must be present in the religious forms in which those people worship. Thus Christian particularism and the identification of Christ with the life, words, and actions of the historical Jesus have often been abandoned in the interest of upholding a view of religion that is universal in scope.

The biblical writers insist that these religions cannot be viewed in so innocent a light. They are the futile and perverse response of fallen human beings to God's general revelation. There is no God corresponding to the god of these religions (Isa. 44:9-20; 1 Cor. 8:4-6). Pagan worship is generated in sin (Rom. 1:25) and is a violation of the first commandment. However benign it may be in its appearance, whatever good it may do, it is an affront to God. It brings men and women into relationship not with the triune God who has revealed himself in nature but directly or indirectly with the demons that inspire idol worship (1 Cor. 10:19-22).

Nevertheless, it is important to affirm that God in his sovereign freedom can choose whom he will to be recipients of his revelation or grace, and that he has not always restricted himself to his covenant people. Abraham was blessed of Melchizedek (Gen. 14:18-20). Others received dreams (Abimelech in Gen. 20:6-7) or revelations (Pharaoh in Gen. 41:25; Nebuchadnezzar in Dan. 2:28; 4:2), although these disclosures still needed to be interpreted (Gen. 41:38-39; Dan. 4:18). Jethro sacrificed to God (Exod. 18:12). Do these cases give us grounds for supposing that religions outside of the Judeo-Christian stream have ever been considered acceptable alternatives by God?

The cases we have in the New Testament are instructive in this regard. For example, God revealed his will to the wise men, who were representatives of the Gentiles, leading them by a star and warning them in a dream (Matt. 2:1-12). But there is no indication that they were saved by their religion; instead, God brought them to worship Jesus as their king. Likewise, the Roman centurion had his prayers heard by God and received an angelic visitor. This led Peter to state the principle that "God does not show favoritism but accepts men from every nation who fear him and do what is right" (Acts 10:34-35). However, Cornelius already worshiped the God of Israel, though he was not himself a Jew, and the narrative makes it clear that it was not until he heard the Word and believed that his sins were forgiven and received the Holy Spirit (Acts 10:43-48) that he was accepted by God. That his salvation occurred during Peter's preaching is expressly declared by the centurion himself (Acts 11:14). Thus the assertion that God does not show favoritism is a declaration of his intention to accept men and women from all nations; it is not a declaration of his intent to accept all religions.

There were additional individuals whose preparation for faith occurred outside of God's redemptive history. There were the Ethiopian eunuch (Acts 8:26-39), the Ephesian disciples of John the Baptist (Acts 19:1-7), and perhaps even Paul himself. He met the risen Christ on the Damascus road, but his sins were not formally forgiven and he did not join the disciples until Ananias led him to call upon the name of Jesus and be baptized (Acts 22:16; 9:17-18).

An important conclusion follows from this. Whatever contact these people had with God in their own religious settings was not itself salvific. Their salvation did not occur until they were led to an explicit and conscious faith in Christ through the preaching of the gospel. The claims sometimes made by missionaries that there have always been those in other religions who have worshiped the Christian God need to be evaluated in this light. Religions may play a preparatory role; they may be the means by which men and women seek the biblical God, and God himself may be leading them through their needs and desires. Salvation, however, is not given until the gospel, the message of Christ's dying in the place of guilty sinners, is believed. There is no other way to salvation (Acts 4:12; Rom. 10:8-11). This has always been the basis upon which missionary work has been predicated, for faith can come only through the preaching of God's Word. Therefore, the teaching of God's Word needs to be taken to those who have not heard it (Rom. 10:14-17).

The role of the Holy Spirit in creation and universal history can now be summed up in the following way. The presence of God—Father, Son, and Spirit—in creation and universal history must not be confused with God's work in redemption. The Spirit's presence in the world is not a redemptive presence because it does not address the spiritual death that sin has brought, the slavery to evil spiritual forces that results, or the judgment of God under which all have fallen. It is only through and in conjunction with the preaching of the biblical gospel that the Holy Spirit grants spiritual life, creates faith, emancipates from demonic forces, and brings men and women under the saving grace of God. It is fundamental to biblical revelation, therefore, to preserve this distinction between general and special revelation, common and saving grace, the work of the Spirit in creation and his work in recreation, and law and gospel. Where general revelation is seen to be special, common grace is seen to be saving, creation is seen to have within it the seeds of redemption, and the law is thought to be the gospel, there Christian faith will be destroyed. By contrast, where that which is general is obscured, where common grace is denied in order to enhance that which is saving, where the Spirit's work of regeneration is so stressed that his work of creation is forgotten, there what is prerequisite to saving faith will be lost, and much that God is doing in our world will be obscured. These distinctions must be retained, and at the same time all of these elements must be preserved.

Thus God has so revealed himself in nature and human nature that the failure to know him and to do his will is inexcusable. All have, in fact, sinned. All are in rebellion against God, in slavery to their own sinful selves, and in bondage to a world given over to wrongdoing and controlled by evil forces. The presence of general revelation, of common grace, and of the Spirit himself neither provides the basis for a natural theology that can bring men and women into a saving relationship with God, nor exempts human spirituality from the judgment of God. The Holy Spirit who works in culture generally also works in some people specifically to create faith, effect rebirth, and point them to the only means of deliverance and the only source of hope: the risen and glorified Christ.

Implications

What happens, then, when a person of another faith becomes a Christian? How much of his or her religious culture is left behind, and how much is retained? Some converts are like a man fleeing a burning house: they leave everything behind. Unfortunately, such converts may uncritically embrace Western and secular beliefs and practices to fill the vacuum. One form of idolatry is thus replaced by another. Conversion to Christ must be radical. No one can serve two gods, adhere to two conflicting ideologies, or believe in two value systems. But he or she does have to live with the tension of acknowledging the Lordship of Christ in all of life while maintaining a personal identity within his or her culture. To be a Christian and, say, a Kenyan at the same time involves an ongoing critical evaluation of both identities. It is here that the Holy Spirit becomes our advocate and helper, our guide, revealing the Father's will and protecting us from the Evil One. This process involves change in at least three areas of understanding and behavior.

First, the Holy Spirit will judge and condemn all elements of religious culture that are contrary to the nature of God and his Law. For example, all that is idolatrous, as discussed earlier, is irreconcilable with true religion. Likewise, all forms of the occult, astrology, and magic are forbidden. Covetousness, greed, and sexual perversion are illicit. The whole range of culture—worldviews, aesthetic and moral values, social institutions, customs, and religious life—must come under the searching light of the Holy Spirit, who judges according to the finality of Christ and the authority of God's revealed Word of Truth.

Second, the Holy Spirit transforms and renews all that is good, beautiful, and true in religious culture. Like human life, all of religious life is tainted with sin. No element of culture is left unscathed. All needs to be rejected or transformed in accordance with Christ. Those elements of culture that are not in conflict with God's general and special revelation nevertheless still need the sustaining ministry of the Spirit. For example, marriage and the family belong to the created order and are to be enjoyed by those who live according to the creation principles of Genesis 2:24. John Mbiti of Kenya rightly asserts that the traditional African home, with its strong sense of mutual interdependence and support in time of need, is the center for nurture and education and should be strengthened even further by Christian faith. Similarly, the Hindu joint family has many qualities that make its functioning preferable to the way in which Western nuclear families often function. However, a man's veneration of his mother (even to the point of worship) has to be redeemed so that his wife may take her rightful place in the parental home. Further, the convert may need to deculturize the faith and life-style—whether Western or Third World—that he or she has received from the cross-cultural missionary. All religious faith and culture needs to be refined by the fire of the Holy Spirit in accord with the revealed Word of God.

Third, the Holy Spirit brings to every culture the newness of the gospel arising from the Christ event—Incarnation, Cross, Resurrection, Ascension, and Promised Return. This newness is embodied both in the life of the new believer and in the church as the new society. As the community of the King, the church is distinct from all other communities. The Lord's Supper is the symbol of its unity and life, and the Great Commission is its central mission in the world. The church is the community of the Lord's reconciling grace, of compassionate love for the poor, and of hope for a new earth and a new heaven. But the church is equally the community of the Holy Spirit, who cleanses and empowers for service, and gives spiritual gifts for ministry.

The work of critical reflection upon a culture for the purpose of evangelism requires that missionaries and evangelists who are outside of that culture as well as Christians who belong to it hone their skills in both dialogue and apologetics.

Dialogue is not for the purpose of discovering Christ in other religions, as some in the ecumenical movement contend; it is for the purpose of clearing away misunderstanding. It is a humbling and melancholy fact, for example, that many Muslims evaluate Christianity in the light of the Crusades, which began in the eleventh century, as well as in the light of the recent influx of pornography from the West. Some Africans still find it difficult to separate Christian faith from Western imperialism and slave trading, or from inhumane policies like those of South Africa. These memories and experiences are the breeding ground for suspicions, fears, animosities, and sometimes outright hatred. They need to be explored with care, sensitivity, and humility. Christians need to understand why others feel the way they do, and must be willing to acknowledge sin and injustice where they have occurred. Without this preparatory work of listening, of being open to explore with honesty the misconceptions and grievances that might have developed, the sharing of Christian faith often falls on barren soil.

For too long, apologetics has suffered under the libel that it is triumphalistic in nature or, alternatively, that it is redundant in the task of evangelism. It usually appears triumphalistic only to those who have yielded their commitment to the uniqueness of Jesus, the incarnate Word, and the finality of his Cross, the only means of salvation. It is redundant only to those who are unwilling to accept the biblical injunction to persuade men and women concerning the truth of God.

In the West, secularization is especially prevalent, but it is a phenomenon that is already affecting religions and cultures worldwide. Since urbanization and secularization are almost invariably yoked, and since the world as a whole is moving rapidly toward urbanization, secularization is going to be an even greater factor in the future. The results that secularization produces are already known. It de-Christianizes, de-divinizes, de-demonizes. Through its alliance with technology, it forces upon us a unidimensional view of reality; it forces us to think of the world and of ourselves as divorced from any divine reality. It cuts us loose from absolutes and therefore demands, in their place, that all religions be viewed as possible ways to God.

The experience of this pluralism erodes confidence in the finality and uniqueness of Christ. It also locks up in the prisons of doubt many in urban and technological societies—both Eastern and Western—who have been conditioned to disbelieve in the supernatural and to deny the authority of the Bible. The very contention that all truth is relative to the person or culture holding it is the very means of self-deprivation, for this contention is itself the barrier to belief.

In such contexts, the need for apologetic work is very great. The presuppositions of unbelief need to be exposed, its outworkings challenged, its results highlighted. And Christian faith as an alternative worldview, the only faith that both meshes with reality and explains human experience, needs to be presented. This is not itself the presentation of the gospel, but it is the preparation for that gospel. It is a work that the Holy Spirit has greatly blessed and used in the past; it is a work calling for believers to undertake it. Can the evangelical church rouse itself to meet the challenge? Are there men and women who are willing to read, study, think, and discuss in order to forward the faith? Are there those who will give of themselves in the service of Christ to accomplish this goal?

Chapter III
The Gospel Made Effective

Our vastly increased knowledge of the size of the world today, of its cultural diversity and its linguistic complexity, has put the Great Commission in a new light. Christians who have read their Bibles have always known that Christ commanded his followers to go into all the world with his message; it is what this command entails that has now become clearer than ever before.

Indeed, given modern circumstances, the finality and comprehensiveness of the Great Commission are daunting. In many parts of the world today, for example, doors are closed to Christian missionaries. In others, Christians meet and profess their faith at great danger to themselves. Not only so, but unbelief often appears invincible, and cultures whose values are not even remotely Christian appear to be impenetrable. In short, the prospects for success seem minimal. How is it possible that we will be able to take the gospel of Christ's forgiveness to the whole world?

Of course, the answer to this question is many-sided, but it is certain that the task will be doomed from the start unless we properly understand the role of the Holy Spirit in this enterprise. Outside of the supernatural working of God's Spirit, unbelief is invincible, cultures are impenetrable, and doors are closed. The questions we need to consider, then, are how the Holy Spirit works and what he does. In order to do this, we will need to think about three matters. First, what was the relation between Jesus and the Spirit? Second, what is the relation of the Spirit to Christ's work on the Cross? And third, how does the Spirit enable us to preach this gospel with efficaciousness worldwide?

Jesus and the Spirit

From start to finish, the Holy Spirit was intimately associated with the life of Christ. This intimate association is indispensable to our presentation of Christ in the world today.

Both Matthew and Luke explicitly declare that the Holy Spirit was the agent by whom the Incarnation occurred (Matt. 1:18-21; Luke 1:35). They speak of Christ's conception with great delicacy, but their records nonetheless offend some modern theologians. Even today, crude scenes of gods mating with humans are conjured up; it is presumed that this is what the gospel writers envisioned. This presumption, however, is without foundation. What is taught in the birth narratives is not the manner of Jesus' conception but its agency. The Holy Spirit, life-giver and creator, produced supernaturally within and through Mary that sinless humanity with which the Word could be bonded in personal union.

Jesus' ministry was inaugurated by the Holy Spirit at his baptism, thus signaling to Jewish observers in particular the arrival of the messianic age that they had been seeking. The Holy Spirit, who had been the agent of Jesus' birth, presumably had already been active in his growth into maturity; now Jesus' mission was seen to be Spirit-initiated and Spirit-oriented. The same Spirit through whom he was conceived, baptized, and anointed would be his divine guide in temptation (Matt. 4:1; Mark 1:2) and his divine agent in exorcisms (Matt. 12:18, 24-32; Mark 3:22-30). By the Spirit, Jesus would demonstrate the power of God in his mighty miracles, the authority of God in his proclamation, and the will of God in his death. It was, we are told, by the "eternal Spirit" that Jesus gave himself in our place as a sacrifice for sin (Heb. 9:14) and by the same Spirit that he was raised from the dead (Rom. 8:11). So it is that Jesus' birth, baptism, miracles, teaching, sacrifice, and resurrection are all ascribed to the working of the Holy Spirit.

One of the main concerns of John's gospel, with which we may bracket his letters, is personal communion with God, which is referred to as "eternal life" or simply "life" (John 17:3). Thus John's interest in the Spirit who rested on the incarnate Son (1:32-33; 3:34) centers on the fact that following Jesus' departure (death, resurrection, ascension), the Father and the Son would send the Spirit to the disciples to be the second Paraclete (Counselor, Helper, Advocate, Adviser, Ally, Supporter, Encourager) in Jesus' place. In his ministry as Paraclete, he would make Jesus, and with and through him the Father, consciously present to the disciples (14:16-24), and also make the full truth about Jesus clear to them, partly by causing them to remember and understand what Jesus had said while he was with them, and partly by additional revelation (14:26; 16:13). "He will bring glory to me," Jesus said, "by taking from what is mine and making it known to you" (16:14). And through the richness of this new revelational experience, the disciples would find that it was to their advantage that Jesus had left them (16:7). The Spirit's ministry as

Paraclete would have an evangelistic significance, too, for he would convince the world of the truth about Jesus. In John 16:8-11 Jesus speaks of this ministry and promises that the Spirit will convince the world of sin, righteousness, and judgment. In 1 John 2:20-27, 4:1-6, and 5:6-10a, the apostle looks to the Spirit to attest to the truth of the Incarnation against Gnostic Docetism, with its consequent denial of sacrificial atonement and propitiation by blood. The Spirit acts as the Spirit of truth, vindicating the reality of the incarnate Son as our mediator, sin-bearer, and source of life against all forms of misbelief and denial. This is his work as *witness* (John 15:26; 1 John 5:7-8).

Given the intimate relation between the Holy Spirit and Jesus in the Synoptic Gospels and the subsequent extension of the ministry of Jesus in the world, it is no surprise to note how the language about the Holy Spirit begins to change in other New Testament books. There he is referred to as "the Spirit of Christ" (Rom. 8:9; 1 Pet. 1:11), "the Spirit of Jesus" (Acts 16:7), "the Spirit of Jesus Christ" (Phil. 1:19), and "the Spirit of his Son" (Gal. 4:6).

We have seen that the Holy Spirit miraculously created within Mary the humanity to which the Word was joined in personal union; that the Spirit came upon Jesus in baptism, signaling the inauguration of the messianic age; that the Spirit filled Jesus, led him in his ministry, and sustained him in his temptations; and that it was by the Spirit that Jesus surrendered himself in substitution for us at the Cross, and by the Spirit that he was raised from the dead. The Holy Spirit—who was so intimately associated with the whole of the life, death, and resurrection of Christ—is the one who has interpreted, finally and infallibly, the meaning of these acts. God's acts in history are not self-interpreting; they need to be interpreted. And the Holy Spirit has so interpreted them for us by inspiring the Scriptures (2 Tim. 3:16). He utilized responsible human agents to write in such a way that, while their style and thought are preserved, what they wrote corresponds exactly to what God wanted to communicate. What the Scripture says, God says.

In the New Testament, then, the biblical Word and the work of the Spirit are correlated. It is not possible, in biblical terms, to believe in the Holy Spirit's work without believing in the Bible's inspiration, for the biblical revelation is the Holy Spirit's written witness. Nor is it possible to understand the full truth of Scripture and to receive what God wants us to receive unless the Holy Spirit who inspired the Word also leads us in our understanding of it. This relationship between the objective and the subjective needs to be carefully preserved. The Holy Spirit neither leads nor teaches anyone in ways that are contradictory to Scripture, for then he would be leading and teaching in ways contradictory to the clear written will of God. By the same token, the Scriptures are not merely ancient documents, nor are they merely the products of their human authors. By confluent action, the Spirit employed human authors to deliver the revelation of God in, with, and through human language. It is his work to respeak these words to succeeding generations, making their truth decisive, urgent, and contemporary. Scripture therefore needs to be studied and heard in humble dependence upon God the Holy Spirit, who first inspired it. Word and Spirit must be held together and experienced together; if they are not, our retention of biblical Christianity will be jeopardized. The saving knowledge of God is not a knowledge given within nature or human experience. It is one communicated through Word and Spirit together, the God-sent Spirit opening the God-given Scriptures with clarity and bringing conviction, thus making the divine origin and meaning of the Bible clear to us, and focusing our attention upon Christ, the incarnate Word.

This being the case, we have some basic criteria for testing religious claims. No claim to knowing and experiencing Christ can be accepted if the Christ so known and experienced has been cut loose from the life, teaching, death, and resurrection of Jesus. No leading of the Spirit can be accepted as the leading of the Spirit of Christ if it does not bring us toward him, does not confront us with the uniqueness of his life and death and call for our obedience to him. No truth can be accepted as mediated by the Spirit if it does not conform to and originate in the teaching of Scripture.

All of these criteria, however, should also be expressed positively. There is an intimate and unbreakable relation between the Word living and the Word written. And it is the Holy Spirit who is the eternal link between the life, death, and resurrection of Jesus (the divinely interpreted meanings of which are given in Scripture), and men and women in succeeding ages who need to understand these things. The Holy Spirit opens their minds to understand the truth he has provided in Scripture in order that they might worship and serve Christ as their Savior and Lord.

The Cross and the Spirit

Biblical Teaching

The fact that our New Testament authors had to ransack their vocabulary to find words, images, and illustrations rich and diverse enough to describe the work of Christ should warn us against making distinctions

that are overly simple. Nevertheless, it is useful for us to begin by noting
that there is a distinction between what Christ did *for* us and what he does
in us. The former is objective and was accomplished with finality, in
space and time, on the Cross; the latter is subjective, accomplished in the
present by the Holy Spirit, and will be completed only at death or at the
time of Christ's return. What is here distinguished cannot, of course, be
separated. The subjective is based on the objective. The Spirit's work of
applying Christ's death assumes that Christ did indeed die in substitution,
that by giving himself in the place of sinners and exchanging his righteousness for their sin, he conquered for them sin, death, and the devil.
Without this work of Christ on the Cross, there could be no work of the
Spirit in his people.

We need to refine further what we have described as the subjective
work of the Spirit. In the process, however, the category of "subjective"
begins to break down a little. In order to understand the Spirit's work
from another angle, we can think in terms not of Christ's work (with its
distinction between objective and subjective) but of the sinner's experience. When we do this, different distinctions emerge. We can think of the
sinner as the object of God's grace and as the participating subject in it.
This corresponds to sin, which also has a twofold nature. Objectively, sin
is blameworthiness, inasmuch as it is a violation of God's law, and
subjectively, it is destructiveness, inasmuch as it corrodes life and brings
sorrow in its path. Sin is thus both metaphysical and psychological, and
God's grace addresses both dimensions. As the objects of grace, we are
justified; our standing before God is addressed. As subjective participants
in God's grace, we are regenerated and sanctified; our being is renewed
after the image of Christ. Both of these aspects can be further divided, but
for the sake of brevity only a few ideas in the biblical presentation can be
touched upon here.

The most decisive event in the application of God's grace is justification. Justification is, in particular, Paul's special interest, but what he
teaches is completely consistent with John's discussion about eternal life
and Jesus' discussion about the Kingdom. In Paul's mind, this doctrine
captured the essence of Christ's resolution of the sinner's plight before
the law. Justification is a courtroom term. It describes how Christ took the
place of guilty sinners, bearing their sin (cf. Isa. 53:11, 12; Heb. 9:28) and
imputing to them his righteousness (Rom. 3:25; 5:10; 2 Cor. 5:21; Gal.
3:13). Thus, through faith, sinners who are joined to Christ can be viewed
as having kept the law, not because they actually did so but because
Christ did so representatively on their behalf (Rom. 5:12-21). And Christ

is viewed as having sinned, not because he actually did so but because he took our sins as we had committed them and made them his own. He bore our punishment, stood in our stead, and now our guilt is removed, our condemnation revoked (Rom. 8:1), and our alienation from God reversed (Rom. 5:10; cf. Eph. 2:16; Col. 1:10).

Regeneration is that work of the Holy Spirit by which a new nature is formed within a sinner as a consequence of his or her union with Christ. It is spoken of as birth (John 1:13; 3:3-8; 1 Pet. 1:23; 1 John 2:29) or new birth (Titus 3:5; 1 Pet. 1:3), as itself an act of creation (Eph. 2:10), or as something brought forth (James 1:18). This work of the Holy Spirit is radical in nature because there is only death and bondage within the fallen nature. The Spirit creates a breach with all that is past, making a new person with a new nature and new appetites that can be satisfied only in the new habitat of Christ. The Spirit does not simply renovate what is already extant in the sinner. The life of sanctification is not merely what is patched up from the life outside of Christ. The Spirit instead works to create a life *de novo,* imbuing the new being with powerful motives of holiness (Eph. 4:24; Col. 3:10) and sustaining and supporting the new life that he has brought forth.

In John's writings this point is developed distinctively and unmistakably. The Holy Spirit, we are told, draws us inwardly to Christ (John 4:23-24; cf. 17:3). It is in this sense that the Spirit "gives life" (6:63). This "life" belongs to those who see and enter the kingdom of God by putting their faith in Jesus (3:14-18), and the seeing and entering occur only through being born again "of water and the Spirit" (3:3-7). The fact that Jesus censures Nicodemus—"Israel's teacher" and therefore, presumably, a biblical expert—for not knowing how new birth could take place (3:10) suggests that the new birth is a two-word parable of the totally new start that would be effected by the prophesied cleansing and renewing of heart by the Spirit (Ezek. 37:25-27; cf. Ps. 51:10-12). In 1 John the parable has become a theological doctrine in its own right: birth from God, which makes us his children, produces true belief in Christ, righteousness of life, and a loving disposition, and makes habitual sin a thing of the past, because sinning is contrary to our renewed moral nature (1 John 2:29–3:10; 4:7; 5:1, 4, 18). Though the epistle does not explicitly link birth from God, being "of God" (1 John 4:6; 3 John 11), with the Spirit's inward work, Jesus in his speech to Nicodemus clearly equates the Spirit's work with the new birth, whereby one is born of the Spirit (John 3:6).

The Spirit is witness to Christ, maintaining the believer's communion with him so that "streams of living water" (the life-giving, health-giving influences of a transformed life) flow from the believer (John 7:37-39; cf. Ezek. 47:1-12). Not until Christ had triumphed on the Cross (John 13:31-32) and had returned to the Father's side (17:2-5), however, would the Spirit begin work in his role as Paraclete. This had to be so in the nature of the case: the Spirit could not glorify Christ to the disciples by showing them Christ's glory until Christ had entered into that glory, had made it a reality to be shown (16:14). After the Resurrection, Jesus breathed on the disciples and said, "Receive the Holy Spirit" (20:22); but since at that moment Jesus had not ascended to be glorified in the full Johannine sense (20:17), it is better to treat this as an acted promise of what would very soon happen (at Pentecost, about which John's intended readers were not ignorant, any more than John himself was) than to suppose that John means us to gather that the Pentecostal spirit, the Spirit as Paraclete, was actually bestowed in that moment by Jesus' action.

In relation to the individual Christian, then, the Spirit's ministry is fivefold. He *enlightens*, giving understanding of the gospel, so that "the spiritual man" has "the mind of Christ" (1 Cor. 2:14-16; 2 Cor. 3:14-17). He *indwells*, as the seal and guarantee that henceforth the Christian belongs to God (Rom. 8:9-11; 1 Cor. 3:16-17; 6:19). He *transforms*, producing in the believer the ethical fruit of Christlikeness (2 Cor. 3:18; Gal. 5:22-24): love, joy, peace, patience, kindness, goodness, faithfulness, gentleness, self-control, and, we should add, prayerfulness and hope (Rom. 8:26-27; 15:13). He *assures*, witnessing to the believer's adoption by God, to his or her eternal acceptance and future inheritance (Rom. 8:15-25, 31-39, which is a transcript of the Spirit's witness; Gal. 4:6). And he *equips* the believer for service among God's people and in the world (Acts 1:8; 1 Cor. 12:1-31).

Just as the "age to come" overlaps chronologically with this "present age," so the life of the Spirit runs concurrently with and is known alongside and in conflict with the life of the flesh. The Holy Spirit's new creation does not bring immediate deliverance from all of the sins that hitherto we accepted and which we indulged. There is a conflict between flesh and Spirit that is unremitting. To live by the flesh is to live in such a way that we satisfy our fallen human nature and uphold the norms and values of our fallen world. To live by the Spirit is both to live in his power and to cultivate those values and virtues that evidence the presence of the "age to come."

Thus the life of sanctification is a life of conflict between the Holy Spirit on the one hand and, on the other, our fallen nature together with the "world" that is its expression in cultural and social form. Just as spirit and flesh are contrasted, so are faith and the world.

In the New Testament, the word *kosmos* (world) is used in a variety of ways, but there are two main usages that need to be noted and compared. First, it is used of the creation. It embraces the organic universe that God has made, is preserving, and will one day entirely restore. This universe is now subject to the effects of the moral disorder that sin has brought, but the effect of Christ's conquest at the Cross will be cosmic as well as personal. This universe will be so restored and reconstituted that its new heavens and new earth will be the abode of righteousness (2 Pet. 3:13). Despite the bondage into which the earth has fallen, it is viewed in an entirely positive light in Scripture. It is to be enjoyed as God's handiwork; its resources are to be wisely and morally used as gifts; and the life that it sustains is to be protected and preserved and used as a means of glorifying its creator.

But *kosmos* is also used to refer to all of fallen humanity (John 1:29; 3:16; 1 John 2:2), for which Jesus is the only possible savior (John 4:42; 1 John 4:14). It refers frequently to that network of values in a culture that has its origin in human rebellion, values whose focus is the fallen creature rather than the creator, values that make human sinning look normal and desirable. Thus the "world" becomes the cultural and social context in which human alienation from God is institutionalized and normalized (cf. John 1:10; 3:19; 14:17; 15:18).

This world, though alienated from God and refusing Christ's salvation, is nevertheless not devoid of spiritual influences. Behind the organized fabric of fallen human life lies Satan's relentless hostility to God. It is human beings, both in the personal and social dimensions, who are the battleground and the prize in this contest between light and darkness, the Lamb and the dragon, God and the devil. Satan is "the god of this age" (2 Cor. 4:4); he is its "prince" (John 12:31); it is all controlled by him (1 John 5:19).

Men and women who are outside of Christ are not innocents merely suffering from ignorance that can be easily remedied. They are caught in the thralldom of the terrible trilogy of the world, the flesh, and the devil (Eph. 2:2-3). They may not be inhabited by evil spirits, but in their fallenness they are nevertheless controlled by Satan's evil intentions. They are without spiritual life and without the means of extricating themselves from Satan's dominion; without Christ they are without hope.

The work of the Spirit, then, is first to effect a transition from the kingdom of darkness to the kingdom of light, and then to wean Christ's people from their lingering taste for and associations with the fallen world. This work is achieved not only through the Spirit's indwelling, but also by means of the truth of the Scripture, and by the nourishment and reinforcement of the church. The world is the externalization of human rebellion, and therefore every sinner can find in culture those reinforcements to sin that he or she desires. Just so, those who have been renewed in Christ should find in the church a context of holiness and service that reinforces and nourishes the life of the Spirit within them.

Historical Discussion

The Holy Spirit's work in applying the benefits of Christ's death and mediating his grace was, in the early church, usually discussed in the context of the organized life of the church. Although patristic opinion was not uniform, the majority saw baptism as the means of regeneration.

The Constantinopolitan Creed, reflecting a patristic consensus, brought the Spirit's work of creation into close relationship with his work of recreating human lives. Thus it was not unnatural that the image of water in Genesis 1 should suggest the rite of baptism in the church; indeed, the New Testament itself sometimes puts the work of the Spirit in close proximity with baptism (e.g., Acts 2:38; 8:16-17; 10:47; 22:16). Tertullian, for example, noted how life emerged from the waters in Genesis 1 and asserted that it was no wonder "if in baptism waters know how to give life." In both cases, however, life is not in the water itself but in the Holy Spirit, who employs it in his work. The "Spirit immediately supervenes from the heavens," Tertullian said, "and rests over the waters, sanctifying them from Himself; and being thus sanctified, they imbibe at the same time the power of sanctifying."

In the creed the church summed up this belief by confessing "one baptism to the remission of sins." The remission of sins, however, was effected not by the water itself but by the Holy Spirit, whose life, precisely because it is holy, is also the means of sanctification. The church fathers saw baptism as the "laver of regeneration." Through the Spirit the believer dies to sin and is raised to new life in Christ.

In a similar way, the Spirit in his recreating and life-giving work was also associated with the Eucharist. Ignatius declared, for example, that when the eucharistic prayer was said, the Spirit descended, making the bread and wine "the medicine of immortality, the antidote that we should not die, but live forever in Jesus Christ." Out of this belief developed the idea that every congregation should secure a permanently available charismatic to preside at the Eucharist in order to make it effective. Without the Spirit, the sacraments would be empty rites; where the Spirit was absent, the sacraments would cease, at least in practice, to be sacraments.

This proposition was to be severely tested almost two centuries later when Augustine and the Donatists debated the same issue. Augustine began with the Western perception of the church as a charismatic community, but he made some modifications in this tradition. His Neoplatonist beliefs enabled him to make a distinction between the outward action of the sacrament and its inward effect. He therefore claimed that the sacrament had validity regardless of the spiritual condition of the person administering it or of the person receiving it. The Donatists could thus administer the sacraments validly; they could not, however, administer them effectively. The inward effect of the sacrament occurred only within that community within which the Holy Spirit dwelled, and the Spirit dwelled in the Catholic—not the Donatist—Church. In other words, to be effective, the sacraments had to be administered by Catholics.

The line of development from the patristic church to the church of the Protestant Reformation passes through Augustine, the colossus who bestrode both the patristic and the medieval worlds and whose influence registered in the sixteenth century upon both the Reformers and their Catholic opponents. Both his reflection upon the Trinity (previously noted) and his contention with the Donatists over the sacraments related to his view of the experience of grace. He combined elements that Martin Luther later sundered, thus setting the Reformation churches moving down a different road.

Augustine frequently identified the Holy Spirit with love. This enabled him to see the Spirit as being both the means and the aim of our salvation. The Spirit is the means because he is the one who pours divine love into the hearts of sinful men and women, love that enables them to reach the goal of loving God. Accordingly, Augustine defined grace as the infusion of love into human hearts by the Holy Spirit. He reshaped the concept of justification to mesh with this idea. Because of this infusion of love, sinners are transformed and enabled to become just by becoming lovers of God and their fellow human beings. This view precipitated two questions. First, to what extent is justification dependent upon sinners' cooperation with this divine work? In other words, how much of our justification rests upon what God does, and how much rests upon what we do? Second, is this grace actually transmitted through the sacraments, and if so, how?

This second question, of course, continued to spur debate during the Middle Ages, debate that spilled over into the Reformation churches as well. Those influenced by Augustine's Neoplatonism continued to insist that the Spirit can act only on spirit and that matter can act only on matter. The effect of the sacrament, therefore, was separated from the act. Those who opposed this aspect of Augustine's thought argued that the Spirit can act not only on spirit but also on and through matter. Thus the act of the sacrament was made coincidental with the effect. This inherent tension in Augustinian thought between "sacramental realism" and "sacramental spiritualism" was time and again discharged in heated debates between "realists" and "spiritualists," especially with regard to the Eucharist. In the ninth century the debate between Radbertus (a realist) and Ratramnus (a spiritualist) highlighted the Augustinian dilemma; in the eleventh century the debate between Berenger (a spiritualist) and Lanfranc (a realist) once more brought it to the surface. Realism gradually got the upper hand, and the rather un-Augustinian doctrine of transubstantiation established itself.

But the built-in tension in the Augustinian heritage was never completely abolished, and the "spiritual" line of thought again came to light in the late Franciscan doctrine that sacramental sign and sacramental effect are held together only by an arbitrary decision of God. Inherently, sign and effect have nothing to do with each other (Duns Scotus, Ockham).

The first issue precipitated by Augustine's doctrine of grace—namely, the nature of justification—was debated in a way that paralleled the debate over the sacraments. In the High and Late Middle Ages, the Thomist Dominicans carried on the Augustinian tradition by emphasizing the divine initiative and the absolute necessity of infused grace. They thought that the individual was largely responsive in the first stages of the process of justification, and cooperative or supporting in the later stages of the work of grace. The Franciscans tended more toward semi-Pelagianism. They stressed the necessity of the human response, and made much out of the individual's preparation for and participation in the work of grace. When the Catholic Church came to formulate its teaching on this point during the Council of Trent in the mid-sixteenth century, it was the Augustinian-Thomist tradition that won out (through the influence of the Jesuits). The Catholic doctrine of justification was here given its classic formulation. Justification was understood as a lifelong *process* that actually changes the sinner into a righteous person. The power in this process is grace infused into the heart through the sacraments. There can hardly be any doubt that the Catholic Church here formulated and carried on important elements in the Augustinian inheritance.

But there were other aspects of Augustine's many-faceted theology that were blurred rather than clarified by this late Catholic formulation of the doctrine of justification. While Augustine had thought of justification as an ongoing process in the sinner—and not as an imputation to that person of Christ's righteousness—he had nevertheless stressed that grace is basically *monergistic* (that it works independently of any human cooperation). Most of Augustine's medieval disciples believed that the work of grace was more synergistic (that it required human cooperation). It was to become the lot of Martin Luther—himself a monk of the Augustinian order—to bring this line of Augustinian thought to its full and consequent formulation. In so doing, Luther went beyond Augustine to recover the full biblical understanding of justification. It is, he said, God's declaration of pardon through the sin-bearing, substitutionary death of Christ. It is a declaration received by faith and made effective by the Holy Spirit. Justification is a divine declaration, not a human achievement; it is itself the beginning of a Christian life, not its summation or conclusion.

On the eve of the Protestant Reformation, the church was in full possession of the doctrine of the Trinity and, as part of this, of the Holy Spirit's personality and divinity. What was far more problematic was the nature of the Spirit's work. The Protestant Reformation was to address some aspects of the Spirit's work decisively and was to construct fresh and more biblical understandings of the relation between Christ, the gospel, and saving belief. Other aspects of the Spirit's work, notably his relation to the sacraments, would be debated along lines already well-established in the past.

Luther's theology of the gospel emerged, of course, from his own intense struggles over sin, guilt, and forgiveness. Given his powerful and complex personality, his theology was (predictably) dazzling, uncompromising, and vehement. Yet it is not difficult to see emerging in it the motifs that were to characterize all of the Reformers' theology. The Reformers crystallized these motifs into a set of slogans that communicated succinctly and strongly what Reformation theology was about. They believed in justification *sola fide* and denied that human cooperation with grace formed a basis of acceptance before God; in salvation *sola gratia* without the admixture of what humans do as a triggering device for that salvation; in acceptance before God *in solo Christo*, who is our substitute and sin-bearer, the conqueror of sin, death, and the devil, doing what no human being can even begin to do; and in the disclosure of God in *sola scriptura*, which is self-interpreting and whose meaning should not be decided by ecclesiastical authority. Only when these four tenets were acknowledged, the Reformers believed, could glory be ascribed to God alone. These tenets, stated here in a rudimentary way, formed the structure around which the different Reformation theologies were built.

These tenets, of course, were not entirely novel; each had at least some precedent in medieval theology. What was new was the way they were understood in relation to one another and the intensity of the personal knowledge of God, structured by the Word, that resulted. This knowledge necessarily involved a fresh understanding of the work of the Holy Spirit. "I believe," Luther's Small Catechism states, "that by my own reason or strength I cannot believe in Jesus Christ, my Lord, or come to him. But the Holy Spirit has called me through the Gospel, enlightened me with his gifts, and sanctified and preserved me in true faith."

What, then, does the Spirit do? Luther's theology frequently drew a dramatic picture of the world as the battleground for the conflict between good and evil, God and the devil. The Spirit is God's agent in this strife, depriving the devil of his great weapons against us—guilt and fear—and restoring us to God through the work of Christ.

The devil's weapons, however, cannot be destroyed without a deep awareness of sin on the part of the sinner. In a broadside fired against Scholastic theology in 1517, even prior to his more famous Ninety-five Theses, Luther attacked Aristotle as the source of the problem at this point, although the main purveyors were Gabriel Biel and Duns Scotus. They seemed to believe that human beings could by nature choose and will to love God, and that this choosing and willing were the preconditions of salvation. The merit of Christ's death became effective only in those persons who had shown themselves worthy of it by their desire for it. In this disputation—as well as in *The Bondage of the Will,* the massive refutation of Erasmus he later wrote—Luther argued that sinners are not free to so choose but are completely captive to their own sin. Neither the "inclination" nor the will is free to love God; sin has invaded, infected, and affected every part of human nature, turning us into rebels against God, his Word, and his Christ. Nothing precedes grace, Luther declared, except "ill will and even rebellion against grace." Using a graphic image from his refutation of Erasmus, he likened the will to a beast that is ridden by only one of two masters: God or the devil. There are no other options. Thus, since God must initiate the right disposition of the heart, the notion that we can train ourselves into becoming righteous—a notion Luther saw as rooted in Aristotle and mediated through much Scholastic theology— is the worst enemy of grace.

Acknowledging our spiritual bankruptcy and, even more than that, our hostility to God and the corruption of all of our motives even when they are at their best is a necessary precondition for receiving God's saving grace. Without this true self-knowledge, induced by the Spirit and given through the Word of God, there can be no justification. Law must precede gospel. The law is not the gospel, because we do not become righteous by doing righteous deeds. The gospel requires that we first hear the law because it is the law itself that convinces us that we cannot keep its demands. The law exposes our sin but in itself is incapable of expunging that sin. It is only as we see ourselves as sinners trapped in our own sinning, affirming in every sin our defiance of God, helpless to break the cycle of rebellion, that we are ready to hear the gospel of deliverance. And it is only when we have been made righteous through believing the gospel that we can begin to do righteous deeds.

What Calvin said about human depravity followed from Luther's formulations. Calvin knew that as long as people are ignorant of their sin, of its nature and of its consequences, they can understand neither themselves nor God. Nor can they see the tragedy of which they are a part, for creatures who have been endowed with such noble and extraordinary capacities have rebelliously turned away from the God who is the source and satisfaction of those capacities. Calvin therefore took great pains to drive home this sober reality and frequently spoke of human corruption using stark, strong terms such as "rottenness," "vileness," and "rebellion." Only when we own before God our sinfulness and our willing captivity to its desires will we long for redemption from these bonds. To fail at this point is to fail to see our need for redemption. To trust in what we are is to build an insurmountable barrier to true faith in Christ. Calvin put the issue as directly and strongly as Luther did: either we trust in ourselves, or we trust in Christ. There are no other alternatives.

The relation between the Spirit's work in inspiring the Scriptures and his work of enabling us to understand their truth for salvation is evident throughout Luther's thought.

Luther believed that the Holy Spirit who so inspired our Scriptures has limited himself to using the Scriptures to accomplish his work in us. Just as God was incarnate only in Christ, so he has revealed himself only in Scripture. What we read in the text of Scripture corresponds to what someone would have encountered in Jesus the man. Jesus' divine nature was often concealed; he was God incognito. And the divine is likewise hidden in the written Word until, by the Spirit's work, it is revealed to us. Because this divine reality is found only in Scripture, and because God has been incarnate only in the one man Jesus, to whom all of Scripture points, the Spirit has linked himself exclusively to the written Word in bringing us to the living Word. Thus no teaching that does not come through the Scriptures can claim to be from God, and that teaching will not be received as from God unless the Holy Spirit mediates it to us through the Scriptures.

More than that, it is this Word that the Holy Spirit uses to create faith within us. When the Spirit thus creates faith, he also leads us inwardly to Christ, who is the object of that faith. Thus faith for Luther was not merely assent to biblical or ecclesiastical teaching. Nor was faith simply inward disposition, which it has frequently become in contemporary existential thought. Rather, Luther believed that faith is the active appropriation of Christ mediated through the written Scripture by the Spirit. It is not the reward for, the complement to, or even the completion of our desire to seek God. Within sinners there is no such desire prior to grace. Faith is a supernaturally initiated gift without which Christ cannot be believed, justification cannot be effected, Christian life cannot begin, the devil cannot be defeated, and God cannot be honored.

As the Protestant Reformation took shape, it developed in several different directions, and while this essential gospel was at its heart, different interests and emphases emerged.

What was striking about Calvin's soteriology was the way in which he developed it so clearly on a Trinitarian basis, seeing the united actions of Father, Son, and Holy Spirit as being directed at the same people and infallibly securing their salvation. According to Calvin, the Father conceived of salvation and chose some for life, leaving others to die in their sins. The Son was appointed to assume human flesh and to die in substitutionary atonement for those whom the Father had given him in covenant. The Spirit is sent to regenerate them, the elect, so that they might believe. Thus Calvin declared in his *Institutes of the Christian Religion* that "the efficient cause of our salvation is placed in the love of the Father; the material cause in the obedience of the Son; the instrumental cause in the illumination of the Spirit" (3.14.21). Within this divine economy, it is the work of the Spirit to effect the Father's will by bringing those who have been chosen into a faith relationship with Christ.

The Spirit's work, then, can be seen as both internal and external. It is external because the Spirit employs the church, especially its ministry, to accomplish the Father's will. In this connection, the Spirit's work is personal but not individualistic. Calvin could be as scathing as Luther in his denunciations of "fanatics" who imagined they had received secret revelations from the Spirit or who, satisfied with their own private reading of Scripture, disparaged its public ministry. God has established not only the church but also its ministers, Calvin declared, and it is through these ministers, as they preach and teach God's Word, that the Lord offers himself to us. The Spirit's work is also internal because he must recreate our broken spiritual faculties if we are to believe. The gospel is offered indiscriminately to all, but only those in whom the Spirit secretly works respond to it. This desire for Christ leads them willingly, rather than coercively, into trusting him and repenting of their sin. Calvin believed that the internal and external aspects of the Spirit's work were united, for there can be no saving apprehension of truth except as a result of its impartation by the Spirit.

The differences between Calvin and Luther were not about the gospel itself but about the doctrines that grew out of it. Calvin affirmed election unflinchingly because he saw it as the Bible's way of protecting the nature of grace, and he was baffled by the Lutheran discomfort with his teaching. Apparently he held to particular redemption, although he made very few direct declarations to that effect. He willingly affirmed the Scholastic formula that Christ's death was sufficient for all but efficient only for the elect—an affirmation that chagrined some Lutherans, who felt that his use of the formula was misleading. And Calvin resisted Luther's view that baptism is regenerative.

If the magisterial Reformers had rediscovered the Pauline teaching on faith, the evangelical Anabaptists saw themselves as embodying the biblical teaching on discipleship. They saw the Reformers as stressing—indeed, exaggerating—the spiritual status of justification; they believed they were called to proclaim the spiritual process of growth. In this, of course, they were not at odds with the Reformers, because the Reformers also believed in spiritual growth. What distinguished the Anabaptists was their *interpretation* of what that growth entailed. For they were convinced first of all that the church had disappeared, at least during the Middle Ages, and therefore could not be *re*-reformed but had to be established. In addition, they believed that their commitment to holiness required opposition to the state in many of its functions because these were "of the world," and liaisons with them would destroy faith.

These two convictions brought the Anabaptists into conflict with the authorities, both Catholic and Protestant, and the consequent suffering they endured is not a happy chapter in the church's past. Their legacy was twofold. First, their commitment to rigorous self-discipline stood as a powerful testimony to God's grace because they adhered to it at great personal cost. Second, they left behind a remarkable record of concern for mission and gospel preaching. For the evangelical Anabaptists, discipleship implied a responsibility to share not only material goods but also the very message of redemption. To be willing to suffer was to be willing to witness.

At least some of these emphases recurred in the eighteenth-century revival in England. This was, of course, especially true among the Wesleyans, who were interested in Christian perfection and who strongly opposed the Calvinistic understanding of election. What should not be overlooked, however, is John Wesley's deep commitment to the biblical understandings of human depravity, of the gratuitousness of grace, of the indispensability of the Spirit's work of calling, illumination, and re-creation, and of the centrality of justification. Given Wesley's powerful reaffirmation of these themes, it can be argued that his theology was really a permutation within the broader Reformed tradition.

The Protestant consensus, then, can be summed up in the following way. First, without a full-orbed, biblical Trinitarianism, the work of the Holy Spirit either evaporates or becomes extremely obscure. Without a clear understanding of who the Spirit is and what his work is, Christology is affected, as are revelation, regeneration, sanctification, the church, and the dynamic of practical piety. Without the Holy Spirit, the eternal third member of the Godhead, the entire morphology of faith is altered. This alteration does not merely impoverish biblical faith; it destroys that faith. Christian faith without the work of the Holy Spirit is not Christian faith.

Second, the Holy Spirit is the other Comforter, the means by which Christ is now present among his people. The ministry of the Spirit is to apply the work of Christ, to point men and women to Christ, creating in them the capacity to repent and believe. The Holy Spirit does not maintain a ministry independent of Christ. It is not possible to claim with any legitimacy that the Spirit's work has been experienced if we are not as a result consciously and explicitly looking to Christ as our Savior and substitute, our Lord and master. The Spirit's work is to glorify Christ, and if Christ is not glorified in ways that are cogently biblical, then the Spirit has not been at work.

The Holy Spirit, then, must be linked with the Father and the Son, for together they are joined in the same task of saving men and women from sin, death, and the devil. The work of the Spirit cannot be disengaged from the truth of the biblical Word; rather, the Spirit works through the Word to convey its truth, to bring its discipline and deliver its promises to God's people. The work of the Spirit and the work of Christ, therefore, belong together and cannot be separated from each other. For what Christ achieved objectively at the Cross, he now applies subjectively to his people through the Spirit, whose chief work it is to glorify him.

The Spirit and Evangelism

The Holy Spirit—whose presence we have traced throughout Jesus' life and whose work it now is to apply the benefits of Jesus' death and resurrection—is given to the church. John the Baptist declared that Jesus would baptize with the Holy Spirit ("and with fire," Matthew adds) to purge and transform human lives (Matt. 3:11-12; Mark 1:8). We are not told how this will happen or what the results will be; perhaps John himself did not know and so could not say. Jesus later specified one consequence: his disciples would be supplied with words to say when under pressure (Matt. 10:20; Mark 13:11). This foreshadowed the boldness realized in Acts.

Thus, in Luke's story of the birth of the church, we find that his interest is in the Spirit as leader and Lord in the church's mission. Indeed, the Spirit is the chief agent throughout his account, which might well have been called "Acts of the Holy Spirit" rather than "Acts of the Holy Apostles," the traditional Greek title. So we find that Luke highlights the renewal of prophecy through the Spirit (Luke 1:15-17, 41-42, 67; 2:25-28, 36-38; Acts 2:18; 11:27-28; 13:1; 21:4, 10-11); that he continually refers to individuals, from John and Jesus on, as "filled with the Spirit" for faithful and fruitful service (Luke 1:15, 41, 67; 4:1, 14; Acts 2:4; 4:8, 31; 6:3, 10; 7:55; 9:17; 11:24; 13:9; etc.); and that he makes much of the Spirit as a divine gift (Luke 11:13; Acts 2:38; 5:32; 11:17) who gives encouragement, brings joy (Luke 10:21; Acts 13:52), provides guidance and help in decision-making (Acts 15:28; 16:6-10), and inspires the ability to witness for Christ with clarity and boldness (Acts 4:31). Clearly Luke's point in all this is that the Holy Spirit is the supreme resource for the church's life and mission. Only as the Spirit is poured out will there be convincing speech and convinced hearts; only so will the gospel advance and ethical fruit follow; and only through prayer are such results effectively sought (Luke 3:21; Acts 1:14; 4:24-31). These points need to be expanded briefly.

First, it is the Holy Spirit who gives power in evangelism as he glorifies Christ. This point is made repeatedly in the Book of Acts. The sermon Peter preached on Pentecost was one in which Jesus was the focus and the Holy Spirit's ministry of conviction was apparent. He convicted listeners of sin ("you . . . put him to death"; Acts 2:23), righteousness ("But God raised him from the dead"; he is "exalted to the right hand of God"; 2:24, 33), and judgment ("The Lord said to my Lord: 'Sit at my right hand until I make your enemies a footstool for your feet' "; 2:34-35). Those who heard were "cut to the heart" (2:37); on that day, three thousand believed.

Likewise, Peter declared to those who saw the crippled beggar healed that this miracle had been performed because of Christ, not through some personal power of his own (Acts 3:12, 16). Later, when the apostles were filled with the Spirit, they "spoke the word of God boldly," and it was "with great power" that they "continued to testify to the resurrection of the Lord Jesus" (Acts 4:31, 33). The Spirit's ministry was to point men and women to Christ, to open their minds and hearts to believe (cf. Acts 16:14) and then so to magnify Christ that he could only be acknowledged as Lord (1 Cor. 12:3).

Technology has had some adverse effects upon the way people think about evangelism. Technology is concerned with effects and with producing those effects in the most efficient way. It is not concerned with those who devise or use it, nor is it concerned with those who are affected by it, since the tacit operative assumption is that what is efficient is right. If technology can produce its results efficiently, then questions of a moral or a reflective nature become redundant.

It is not difficult to see how easily this mind-set can intrude upon the doing of evangelism. Evangelism can be viewed as a human endeavor whose object is to achieve results in the shortest possible time. And if results, efficiently achieved, can be reported, questions about the character of the evangelist and the means employed to carry out the evangelism seem redundant or irrelevant.

This approach, however, not only departs from the biblical pattern but is positively injurious to it. The character of the evangelist and the means he or she uses must be consistent with the message proclaimed. And the message proclaimed has the power to do its work not because of the evangelist's personality or skills of persuasion but because of the mighty power of the Holy Spirit, who alone is able to turn rebellious sinners into obedient followers of Christ.

Luke's second point is that it is the Holy Spirit's role to lead the church and guide its evangelists in their work. We see this repeatedly in Acts. The Spirit sent Philip to speak to the Ethiopian eunuch (8:29-39) and sent Peter to a Gentile's house (10:19). It was also the Spirit who directed the church at Antioch to send out Barnabas and Paul as missionaries (13:2, 4), and the Spirit who changed their itinerary (16:6-10).

Regarding this last instance, it is not unreasonable to suppose that Paul and his companions had planned their missionary strategy with care and had daily sought the Lord's guidance. Their best judgment was that they should preach in Asia and go on to Bithynia; the Holy Spirit instead directed them to Macedonia. This is a reminder to us that the Spirit's leading may not coincide with our best judgments and that the Spirit's work is sometimes quite unpredictable. We have had numerous reminders of this even in our time.

For example, when the missionaries in China were ejected in 1949, they left behind a church of about a million. In the intervening decades, this church has experienced extraordinary growth. The exact figures are in dispute. Official statistics allow that there are now four million in the church, but there are many more believers outside the organized church. Much of this growth occurred during the worst years of social upheaval under the Red Guards. It appears to be the result of the faithful witness of ordinary men and women empowered and employed by the Holy Spirit. Wherever these Christians were sent—to prison, to labor camps or "banishment areas" (like Tsinghai province in the west of China), or to the depths of the country—they, like the disciples of Acts 8:4, preached the word. And God has validated their witness in extraordinary ways. From a human point of view, China during these years has seemed a most unlikely context for Christian expansion. But God has had other plans, and the result has been an astonishing growth in Christian faith. (See Appendix I, "The Spread of Christianity in China Today.")

Revivals are the springtide of the Holy Spirit. They are his sovereign action. They have often occurred at times when the church was in disarray and when faith was being engulfed by unbelief. Only in this respect are they in any sense predictable. They cannot be brought about by human planning; they are the Holy Spirit's to initiate. It is he who gives extraordinary power to the preaching of the Word, reality to worship, purity to life, and joy to living. (See Appendix III, "The East African Revival.")

Luke's third point is that the blessings, work, and presence of the Holy Spirit are effectively sought only through prayer. It is the Holy Spirit himself who sustains us in prayer and who aids us in knowing God's will (Rom. 8:14, 26), but at the same time, we are commanded to offer prayer for God's people in all seasons, with perseverance (Eph. 6:18). We need to learn afresh how to trust God, to ask of him boldly, for when we do, God acts powerfully in our world. Even the best-laid plans for evangelism falter if God the Holy Spirit is ignored in the endeavor; conversely, even the frailest human instruments can be the occasion for his mighty blessing if we seek God in prayer. Let the church pray afresh that Christ's name will be glorified throughout our world as the Holy Spirit does his convicting, illuminating, and magnifying work!

Chapter IV

God's Message and God's People

The gates of hell will not prevail against the church; that much is clear. In the modern world, however, powerful forces are at work on the church, sometimes eating away at its foundations surreptitiously, sometimes distracting it from its real interests, sometimes attacking it directly and unrelentingly. The church will survive, but it has a fight on its hands.

In the West, the church is struggling with a potent combination of an anti-institutionalism and a virulent secularism, the one militating against church structure and the other against church life. With respect to this anti-institutionalism, it is not easy to distinguish its causes from its effects. Television, for example, is frequently anti-institutional in its function because it bypasses all intermediate structures and appeals directly to the viewer. Speaker and viewer converse personally and intimately with one another—that, at least, is the illusion. Does the ubiquity of television (now turned on for seven hours per day in the average North American home) cause this anti-institutionalism or merely reflect it? And what are we to think of the many developments within Christian faith that ply the channels that lie between denominational structures and local churches? The paradenominational groups, however unwillingly and unwittingly, provide some people with an alternative to the church. The charismatic movement appeals directly to people, cutting across ecclesiastical boundaries, parish lines, and the simple organizational limits of local churches. It unites people of different church affiliations and theological perspectives. Social causes such as abortion and nuclear disarmament have linked protestors who, at an ecclesiastical level, would find little to unite them.

Whatever the explanation for such anti-institutionalism, the effect has not always been comforting to ministers in local churches. Western Christians, nurtured in a womb of affluence, are by instinct consumers. They look for the best deal. The goods that the local church is offering are not always the best on the market. If one's interest is evangelism, then why not turn to television instead and support those who use it to preach the gospel? If one's interest is spirituality, why not join a charismatic group? If one's interest is social involvement, then why not link up with the local Right to Life chapter? The plethora of causes and interests outside the churches, the staggering amounts of money given to these causes, their independence from the churches in many instances—these pose a perplexing problem for the churches. But can the churches really complain if they themselves are not preaching the gospel, are not nurturing spiritual interests, and are not meeting their biblical responsibilities in the world?

In some European countries, the situation is a little different from that in North America. In those countries that historically have had official state churches, a biblical preaching ministry has often been conspicuously absent, and discipline has been virtually unknown. Within the structure of these churches (Norway provides an example), voluntary associations have developed to support the cause of home and foreign missions as well as to provide a context for sound preaching. The members of these organizations, however, have also been faithful and active members of their own local churches. This situation points up a key issue—and a key difference between the situation in countries like Norway and the situation in North America. There paradenominational groups function within the church and undergird it; in the United States they sometimes function in place of the local church and so undercut it. If our support of the church is qualified and grudging (as it often is in North America), if we are unlinking what the New Testament insists on linking, how are we going to reconstruct our doctrine of the Spirit?

In Marxist countries as well as in those countries where a hostile religious ideology is entrenched, the situation is again different. Local churches function only with great difficulty and sometimes are unable to function at all. In other countries, social strife and turmoil have wreaked havoc with church life; in still others, tribalism has made a mockery of Paul's declaration that in Christ the barriers dividing race from race have been destroyed. All of these realities raise an important question: What is God's design for the church? More precisely, What is God's will for the local church in carrying out the evangelistic mandate?

Of course it is the case that God has called men and women to serve him in their vocations in secular life, in their calling to be missionaries in foreign countries, and in a host of other ways that are related only indirectly to the life of the local church. This activity of witness and service is precisely what Scripture requires, and limiting the focus here to the local church is in no way meant to ignore or, worse still, criticize this truth. But since the church has been so battered by the forces of modernity as well as by hostile political and religious contexts, it is useful for us to consider once again how the Holy Spirit should be able to use the church in undergirding and initiating evangelism.

This topic is usually treated rather narrowly. Authors who have addressed it in the past have usually done so either in terms of the missionary vision or in terms of evangelistic strategies and programs. These treatments are entirely proper, for no local church can afford to forget the Great Commission, nor can it neglect its local evangelistic responsibilities. But all of these studies assume the viability of the local church. They assume that it can respond to the missionary appeal and that it has the internal resources to fulfill its evangelistic responsibilities in its own neighborhood. Happily, there are many churches for which these are safe assumptions. Whether these assumptions are universally true, however, even of evangelical churches, is another matter. We surely have to ask ourselves why it is that many Christians—especially Western Christians—are seeking to meet their spiritual needs outside the local church. This is not the first time this pattern has been evident. When European Lutheranism became too muscle-bound in its seventeenth-century Scholasticism, a reaction set in. Through the Pietistic movement, many found spiritual nourishment outside the established churches, although this was immediately channeled back into the churches and provided the vision and energy for much missionary outreach. The same was probably true of English Puritanism, and it was certainly true of the Wesleyan movement in the eighteenth century. (Both Wesleys lived and died as Anglicans.) Nevertheless, in most cases evangelism had to be carried on and spiritual nurture found in channels outside of the local churches. In these instances at least, the reactions were also indictments of the church. The church had lost its spiritual viability.

This is the general problem being addressed here (not the more specific concern of how the local church can support a missionary interest or how it might best do its own evangelism). In order to explore this matter, we will consider, first, how the church is a product of the gospel, and second, how the church should be a model of the gospel.

The Church as a Product of the Gospel

Television has often made gospel preaching an enterprise that is independent of the church. (Indeed, evangelists such as Billy Graham who have insisted upon working with the churches before, during, and after crusades are unusual.) For many people, at least in the West, this separation raises the question of what the relation is between the gospel and the church.

The purpose of God, however, has been clear from the beginning. He called Abraham, justified him, and promised that from the patriarch he would gather together a people (Gen. 12:1-3). Israel was this people insofar as the nation was the channel of divine revelation and blessing, but within it there was a core of those who were in a saving relationship to God not by nationalistic heritage but through grace alone, by faith alone (Rom. 4:1-15; Heb. 11:1-39). They were Abraham's real children (Rom. 9:6-18). This is the line that comes into the church. Thus Jesus declared that there would be "one flock and one shepherd" (John 10:16). Paul tells us that Jesus gave himself "to purify for himself a people that are his very own" (Titus 2:14). They were to be a people made up of Jews and Gentiles, those who were near and far, who would become "one new man out of the two" who would be "God's household" (Eph. 2:15, 19) because they would be Christ's people. The church, then, is this flock, this new man, this household.

The corresponding purpose of the gospel is to bring men and women into saving relationship to Christ and thus to make them a part of this body. The order is important. It is for this reason that the Protestant Reformers felt it necessary to reinforce the scriptural distinction between the visible and the invisible church. The invisible church is that company of men and women who belong to Christ by faith; the visible church is the organized and local expression of that faith. Ideally, the visible and the invisible should coincide; the latter should express itself in the former. In actual fact, this does not always happen. Not all of those who meet with a congregation belong to Christ by faith in him and his death for them on the Cross, and, in the television age, not all who belong to him by faith meet regularly with a local congregation.

We thus need to note and avoid the two extremes that, either in theory or in practice, have resulted. According to traditional Roman Catholicism, there was no distinction between the visible and the invisible church. In order to belong to Christ, one had to join the church. The church and its sacraments in particular were the only means Christ provided for the channeling of his saving life. Outside of the church and its established means of grace there could be no salvation. In the 1950s this position began to be modified in practice in some Western countries (though in few places in South America), and in the mid-1960s the Second Vatican Council significantly altered the conception. The pendulum now shifted to the opposite extreme: salvation was made dependent not on the objective ecclesiastical means but on subjective disposition. Thus the Catholic Church deemed it possible not only for those in non-Christian religions to be saved but also for atheists to be saved, provided they responded ethically to the grace within them. This shift in thinking, deleterious in some respects, has been advantageous in others. It has made possible many expressions of those aspects of the religious life shared by evangelically minded Catholics and their Protestant counterparts.

In contrast to traditional Catholics, evangelical Protestants have all too often been detached from the local church. They have stressed the invisible church at the price of the visible. However unwittingly, they have made faith in Christ necessary but the relation to Christ's people somewhat optional.

If traditional Roman Catholicism has confused church and gospel, evangelicalism has sometimes divorced them. In the former we have had an ecclesiastical context without the gospel; in the latter, the gospel has been too isolated from its visible expression and embodiment in the church.

We can now propose a brief working definition of the church. The church, though universal in its scope inasmuch as it includes all who have believed on Christ in all ages, is also local in its expression inasmuch as each congregation is to be a microcosm of the whole. The church, therefore, is that company of men and women who gather together around Christ as their head, to whom they are joined by faith, for the purposes of worship, teaching, fellowship, and witness. This being the case, there can be no church without the gospel, because without the gospel there can be no faith in Christ (Rom. 10:8-15). The gospel creates the church; the church does not create the gospel.

This means that the church is not simply an organization, and it is certainly not a club for those with religious interests. It does have a structure, and it does need to have elders (sometimes called bishops), pastors, deacons, and perhaps other officers who assume particular responsibilities in it. However, the structure and the activities that it generates are not ends in themselves; they are always and in every case the means to an end. That end is the worship and service of Christ. Where the life of the local church becomes the real object of its existence, where it lives only to serve or perpetuate itself, calamity is always close at hand. This kind of calamity is not, as some Protestants imagine, the peculiar affliction of Roman Catholics; it strikes Protestants as well.

It is interesting to contrast the community of Jesus as it is discussed in the Gospels—it is referred to almost entirely in Kingdom language rather than by the later and more organizational name of the church—with the alternatives in that society. The Zealots were the revolutionaries, the makers of holy war, who thought that God's reign would break upon the world through their guerrilla action. In this they were the forerunners of those proponents of liberation theology who have chosen to allow for and participate in violent revolution. The Sadducees, by contrast, argued that compromise with the Roman authorities was preferable to violent assault, which in their opinion accomplished nothing significant. They were therefore very much a part of the political structure and made compromises with its values. The Pharisees both despised the Sadducees' compromise and repudiated the Zealots' violent involvement. They withdrew psychologically and spiritually from their world. And if they should happen to make illicit contact with this world, spiritually or physically, elaborate cleansing rituals were at hand.

What is perhaps most significant about these groups is that their eschatology was actually an apocalyptic doctrine. They all saw the time line as bisected. "This age" would be separated from "the age to come" by the Messiah. The arrival of the Messiah would be the arrival of "the age to come." But this was a future event. The present was given over to the reign of unrighteousness. Clearly a certain hopelessness marked this perspective.

In the teaching of Jesus, however, the Kingdom is the reign of God in the people of God. More than that, it is the arrival in the present of those supernatural conditions that the Jews associated with "the age to come." This messianic age, of course, has not arrived in its completeness, and so we are instructed to pray for its fuller realization (Matt. 6:10; cf. 24:14; 25:31-46). Nevertheless, "this age" is made redemptively effective through Christ's death (2 Cor. 5:17; Gal. 4:4), and because of his resurrection, the power and gifts of the Spirit are given to Christ's people (1 Cor. 12:1-31; 2 Cor. 1:22). In the church, the major *locus* of the Kingdom, "the powers of the coming age" are experienced (Heb. 6:5). And in this experience lies the answer to the violence of the Zealots, the compromise of the Sadducees, and the apathy of the Pharisees of all ages. The church is a new community whose radical nature arises not from its ideology or political program but from its inner moral-religious dynamic. The people of God, who organizationally constitute the visible church, are experiencing and making known that messianic rule for which the Jews longed. It is not a rule merely relegated to the future but one that is penetrating and transforming the present.

Thus there is a sense in which it is not only proper but necessary to speak of the "otherworldly" aspect of the church's life. Without it, there is no realization of "the age to come," no Kingdom, no rule ꞓf Christ, no divine presence experienced. Without it, the church is simply an organization for the discontented, the apathetic, or the socially withdrawn. But *because* it is "otherworldly" in its nature, it must be "this-worldly" in its service and in the exercise of its moral responsibilities. Because it is "otherworldly" it can be effective in its "this-worldly" life. It is this last point that now needs to be explored more fully.

The Church as a Model of the Gospel

The gospel is the message of Christ's salvation; the church is its most important corporate expression. The truth about Christ and his death, therefore, should find tangible expression in the church. Thus the gospel that created the church should also be modeled by the church.

Such modeling is silent proclamation. It has three important aspects: first, the realization of unity; second, the expression of holiness; and third, the experience of the truth and presence of God in worship. Each of these aspects expresses something vital to the understanding of the gospel.

The Realization of Unity

The logic of New Testament thought is beguiling in its simplicity. The unity of the church is something created by Christ; it cannot be achieved by human engineering. The unity of the church is the unity it has in the Father, the Son, and the Holy Spirit. For if there is only one Father, there can be only one family; if there is only one Lord, there can be only one faith, one hope, and one baptism; if there is only one Spirit, there can be only one body (Eph. 4:4-6). This unity, created by and in Christ, must be preserved. It is preserved by holding firm to the biblical truth about him (Eph. 4:14) and by tenaciously preserving the life of love (Eph. 4:15) that the Spirit has given (Rom. 5:5). Speaking "the truth in love" should be the goal of mature Christians. Wherever Christian truth is compromised in the church and wherever Christian love is violated, there immaturity is present and Christ is inadequately modeled.

Christian unity is a revolutionary ideal. It means that in the church men and women should see expressed the healing of those wounds that all societies inflict upon themselves. In Paul's time, the enmity between Jew and Gentile was often intense. Paul declared that this enmity was destroyed in Christ (Gal. 3:28; Eph. 4:4; Col. 3:11) and that the church should express this reconciliation (Eph. 2:15-16). Barriers between men and women, between slaves and free, between cultured and uncultured, and between one race and another must be destroyed and shown to be destroyed. The very fact that in the church disparate groups—men and women, the powerful and the powerless, the dominant ethnic group and the minorities, those at the beginning of life's pilgrimage and those at the end—should be able to find and express a common life is itself prophetic witness; it is also modeling what the gospel is about. Christ's purpose is to draw many, "from every tribe and language and people and nation," into one. They are now and will forever be "a kingdom and priests to serve our God" (Rev. 5:10). And this is what we find already in the early church. An uneducated fisherman like Peter and an erudite, trained Pharisee like Paul, a nobleman like Manaen (the foster brother of Herod Antipas) and a slave like Onesimus, a Zealot like Simon and a despised tax-collector like Matthew, a prisoner like Paul and the members of the imperial guard, Jews and Gentiles, men and women—all found acceptance in the church. They who had been called to faith in Christ were accorded their proper place among Christ's people.

Great preaching has been defined as the ability to rescue familiar truths from the congregation. The unity of the church and the universality of the gospel are truths so familiar that in many instances they have lost their power to grip and reform us. They need to be rescued, to be grasped afresh so that their revolutionary impact is felt once again.

In the United States, blacks were once forced to worship by themselves because all too often they were unwelcome in white churches, and because in their own churches they found sanctuary from the humiliations they experienced in society. Even today there are numerous denominations that are entirely made up of black churches. In South Africa, apartheid laws forbid the kind of expressed acceptance of all races that is effected in Christ and that needs to be modeled in the church. Christians lose their credibility if they accept perceived social demerits as grounds for not welcoming those of other races into the church, because neither merits nor demerits are the grounds of our acceptance by Christ. This gospel of acceptance by God through Christ cannot go hand in hand with a gospel of exclusion from the church.

The "homogeneous unit principle," used as a strategy for church growth, is useful in explaining why some people come to faith. It can be a tool for evangelism. But many evangelicals are apprehensive about using this tool when it comes to church planting. (See Appendix II, "The Spirit and People Groups.") Undoubtedly, those of the same racial or tribal origin and those of the same social and economic standing feel most comfortable with one another in the church. Undoubtedly, they are in a good position—perhaps the best position—to take the gospel to their friends who share their outlook in so many ways. Nevertheless, the church should not be simply a gathering of like people. It should express diversity, not homogeneity, for then it is expressing the real intentions of Christ. He is not the Savior only of the rich in North America, of the poor in South America, of the whites in South Africa, or of the blacks in other parts of Africa. The appeal of the gospel is universal, and the church should be living this truth. Where this is happening—where believers are repudiating the invidious habit of ascribing more worth to some than to others because of race, wealth, or social standing—the church is providing a context of authenticity in which the gospel becomes credible.

The Expression of Holiness

Holiness has been a conspicuous interest among evangelicals because it is a conspicuous interest in the teaching of the New Testament. It is true that the process of sanctification, of which holiness is the result, has generated debate. How much of sanctification can be ascribed to divine agency and how much to human effort? How much of holiness is simply the result of "letting go and letting God," and how much is the result of active dedication? How much of it is internal self-discipline, and how much is external involvement? How much of it is obedience to the law, and how much is owed to emancipation by the Spirit? Is sanctification a single ongoing process or a two-stage process? Is sin a lifelong affliction, or is it possible to experience complete freedom from it?

These questions all have to be addressed if we are to determine what it means to be sanctified. Our focus here, however, is not on the process and the questions it raises but on the results. However these questions are answered, there is no disputing what the practical consequences should be. Holiness is to be our pursuit (Heb. 12:14), our walk (Eph. 5:3). In this we must persevere (1 Tim. 2:15). For the body of Christ is to preach, live, and exhibit a radically different moral life from that of the world around it. It is for this reason that Scripture never presents conversion as a slow and natural growth into a different life-style. It always shows conversion to involve a radical breach, a breach divinely initiated and explicable only upon the basis of Christ's work and the Spirit's regeneration. Once we were in darkness; now we are in light. The conclusion is that we should "live as children of light" (Eph. 5:8). We are to model the values of the new community in Christ. We are to be people of internal purity and external integrity, people whose minds and hearts are governed by the truth of God's Word and whose lives exhibit the fruit of the Spirit (Gal. 5:22-24). We are to live in such a way that our lives contradict the slogans of our age.

In the industrialized, secularized countries of the West, for example, our unregenerate "common sense" assumes that life consists in the abundance of material things possessed, that those who cannot compete in a free enterprise system are of little value, that domination of others is the key to success, that what is efficient is right, that values are never durable or absolute but relative to each person, that God is not meaningfully related to the stuff of everyday life, and that personal peace and prosperity are the real objects of living. These norms, these unarguable propositions are contradicted in the most profound way wherever biblical holiness is present. The church needs to contradict these propositions in words and actions because the church is where Christian holiness must be manifest. Any unbeliever coming into the church needs to know the kind of life to which the gospel summons people, the alternative to which belief in Christ leads.

Each person's experience of the church has both personal and corporate dimensions. The church is experienced personally insofar as it is the individual who has to be regenerate, exercise faith, and serve Christ with the abilities and gifts that he or she has. The church is experienced corporately inasmuch as it offers communal activities such as worship, hearing the Word of God, celebrating the Lord's Supper, witnessing baptism, and serving in the community. Holiness is likewise both personal and corporate. It has to do with individual attitudes, values, and actions; it also has to do with the corporate expressions of these attitudes, values, and actions.

There is nothing novel in what has been said here, but there is much that is revolutionary. Orthodoxy has made some believers strangely complacent about the status quo. This was so even in the New Testament. James records the case of a church that happily embraced the accepted social determinations of who was important and who was not. One day, he tells us, two men entered the church. The one was affluent and socially prominent; the other was poor and beyond the fringes of acceptability. The first was given a seat of honor, and the second was offered the floor (2:1-12). James chided the Christians for so fawning over the rich and powerful (2:5, 6). Apart from any other consideration, he said, this sort of behavior made no sense because the rich and powerful (as was their wont and custom) were all too often abusing the not-so-rich and not-so-powerful in the church. A hint of the same kind of enculturation is evident in the Corinthian correspondence. Here were Christians who longed to be accepted by those "in the know." They wanted to be part of the elite. Paul had to remind them that very few among them were blue bloods, and besides, worldly sophistication meant nothing to God (1 Cor. 1:26-31). Later on, Paul had to address the catastrophic compromises that those in the church had made in terms of sexual values. They had become so accustomed to the sexual looseness for which Corinth was renowned that they had taken in stride an instance of incest in the church, acting as if nothing of moral significance had occurred (1 Cor. 5:1-5).

Orthodoxy in matters of belief is not a substitute for holiness in life, either for the individual or for the church, because orthodoxy in biblical terms includes the moral outcome of that right belief. The church, however, has frequently separated what the Bible has insisted on holding together. Early on in Protestant church life, Martin Luther complained about those pastors who preached so beautifully about Christ's grace and forgiveness and then chose not to draw the practical lessons therefrom. He claimed that they were fine Easter preachers but very poor Pentecost preachers because they were preaching Christ without and, indeed, against the Holy Spirit. It is always so when doctrinal rectitude spares us from the rigors of daily discipleship. The work of Christ and the work of the Spirit are thus divorced. But what has been argued insistently in these pages is that we, like the New Testament authors, must integrate the two, for they are an indissoluble and essential unity. The work of Christ is experienced only through the work of the Spirit, and the work of the Spirit is principally to create a breach with our sinning from the past and to create within us that holiness by which we will love God and our neighbor.

In the early church, Justin Martyr spoke about the moral changes that regeneration should effect:

> We who formerly delighted in fornication, now embrace chastity alone; we who formerly used magical arts, dedicate ourselves to the good and un-begotten God; we who valued above all things the acquisition of wealth and possessions, now bring what we have into a common stock, and communicate to everyone in need; we who hated and destroyed one another, and on account of their different manners would not live with men of

a different tribe, now, since the coming of Christ, live familiarly with
them, and pray for our enemies, and endeavour to persuade those who hate
us unjustly.

Martyr and the other Christians were living in an environment that was
hostile to Christian faith, but even their enemies such as Galen, Lucian,
and Celsus acknowledged the reality of their Christian lives. These antag-
onists could not ignore what had become common practices for these
Christians: love and prayer for enemies, the sharing of possessions, the
repudiation of greed, care for the poor, honesty and reliability in commerce, strict monogamy, discipline in sexual matters, the repudiation of
incest and pederasty, and the rejection of abortion and infanticide. These
believers also showed a remarkable courage in the face of death. In the
modern church, similar witness is borne. In the Soviet Union, for example, an official investigation into rising Christian influence produced four
conclusions. First, Christians are often trustworthy workers and are given
positions of high responsibility. Second, the alcoholism that plagues the
Soviet Union is a problem that Christians seem to have overcome among
themselves. Third, they maintain peace in their family relations and are
even instruments of peace among families in their neighborhoods. Finally, Christians let no one die without consolation, and their conduct is a
powerful source of witness.

These two examples, one from the early church and the other from the
modern church, remind us of the high calling that comes through faith in
Christ. It is a high calling in terms of both privilege and responsibility. It
is the responsibility of our churches to realize corporately, in word and
deed, that life of purity whose origin is in the Holy Spirit and whose basis
is in the work of Christ. In the church gathered around its Lord the gospel
can be lived eloquently, for the moral efficacy of Christianity is a powerful argument for its truth. *Verba docent, exempla trahunt:* Words teach,
examples draw.

The Practice of Worship

In those countries where secularization is dominant, worship may not
seem like a promising context for evangelism. We imagine the secular
person to be a blasé sophisticate who is too caught up in the pleasures of
life to bother with religion. But this is only a part of the picture. And even
those who fit the description are also people who are sometimes afflicted
by pain, troubled by the meaning of their own existence, and who in

moments of somber reflection also contemplate the inevitability of their death. In many cases they are also ignorant of the church, and therefore worship may be a matter of curiosity to them. In England today, "celebration evangelism" is sometimes used as an effective means of communicating the gospel to such people. Celebration evangelism is a combination of praise, testimony, drama, music, and preaching, all of which takes place in an atmosphere of worship. Periods of worship are lengthy (when compared with traditional evangelistic services) because proponents believe that "God inhabits the praises of his people." The assumption is that non-Christians who come into an atmosphere of worship and see the joy of the worshipers will be more prepared to hear God's Word.

We need to note, of course, that the object of worship is not to win unbelievers to Christ but rather to praise and glorify God. God—Father, Son, and Holy Spirit—is the center and focus of worship. Worship is showing forth God's worth. It is a gathering of his people for nothing less or other than this. The Holy Spirit, who is the Spirit of truth, leads us to understand God as he has disclosed himself in Scripture and then to stand in his presence with love, awe, and humility. Here, however, we need to focus on three aspects of the Spirit's work in relation to the Word of God, two of which occur within worship and one that is tangential to it.

First, the preaching of God's Word is a necessary part of worship because in his Word God discloses his character, his will, and his ways, and in our worship we acknowledge him for who he is and what he has done. Not surprisingly, in Luke 4:18 and 43 Jesus identified himself as a preacher, a preacher of good news to the poor, and in Matthew 28:19-20 the apostles were commissioned to be preachers or teachers of his message. Also, in the New Testament churches, the Holy Spirit enabled and gifted people to fulfill preaching responsibilities.

It is possible that the political figure of the herald in the ancient world suggested to the apostles some parallels with the preacher. Both the herald and the preacher came in the authority of another with a message other than their own. Yet the apostles used the noun sparingly (1 Tim. 2:27; 2 Tim. 1:11; 2 Pet. 2:5) but the verb commonly. The point is that in the church it is not the office of the preacher that is so important but the activity of preaching. Preaching is not primarily an ecclesiastical function but a spiritual event.

Preaching is that event in which God respeaks the words of Scripture, making their truth urgent, decisive, and contemporary. Preaching that is disciplined by the nature of Scripture as inspired is therefore that kind of exposition in which God's truth is made so clear and memorable that it is lodged firmly in the hearts of those who hear it. The truth of Scripture is never set out on a take-it-or-leave-it basis, but—if Paul is a model—proclaimed with pleading and wooing, with love and toil, day and night (1 Thess. 2:9). There is nothing foolish about preaching; it is the so-called foolishness of what is preached—namely, Christ—that saves (1 Cor. 1:20-25).

This kind of preaching has had a checkered career. It declined rapidly after the first century and disappeared almost entirely during the Middle Ages, but it was recovered at the time of the Reformation. Luther declared that God lives in the preacher's mouth, by which he meant that God addresses us in command and promise through the preached Word. Calvin marveled at how God deigns to make his voice heard through the stammering tongue of the preacher. In fact, preaching displaced the Catholic magisterium in the Reformation churches, which is why the Anglican bishop John Jewel said that the knowledge of Scripture is the key to the Kingdom.

But preaching began to decline again in the following century. Biblical sermons were often replaced by Scholastic rhetoric. In the Scandinavian Lutheran churches of the seventeenth century, sermons were often so boring and sometimes so learnedly incomprehensible that congregations developed the habit of rearranging the pews so that they could attend to their own business while the preacher was engaging in his! Laws had to be passed prohibiting this practice. Indeed, in the eulogy given at John Gerhard's funeral, it was noted that never once had he been caught napping during a sermon, an observation that was offered as evidence of his very great piety!

Pietism was a reaction to this situation in Europe. It borrowed quite heavily from Puritanism in England, where once again the centrality and spirituality of preaching had been rediscovered. These same convictions also crossed the Atlantic and surfaced intermittently during moments of spiritual recovery in the centuries that followed, but the exposition of God's Word from the pulpit has not had a happy history in America. Toward the end of the nineteenth century, of course, the Bible itself came under fire in America as it had earlier in Europe. Wherever Protestant Liberalism has been dominant, the sermon has usually been the occasion simply for the preacher to speak about his or her consciousness of God or perhaps to offer a moral homily. The dismissal of biblical inspiration has meant the loss of that work of the Spirit by which illumination is given to the biblical Word and God again addresses those who hear it in and through its words.

In the twentieth century, the expository sermon has been assailed by two new forces. First, there has been the impact of psychology. The result is that people have become especially interested in discovering themselves and in improving their self-image and their sense of self-worth. Experiencing the truth through relational channels, through people, is therefore opposed to and made preferable to hearing it through verbal channels. That being the case, preachers feel great pressure to use the biblical text simply as a means of sharing their own personal religious consciousness with the congregation. Indeed, in many churches the sermon is often replaced altogether by either dialog or drama. Second, preaching has been assailed by those who distinguish between "hot" and "cold" media. They think that the printed and the spoken word are virtually passé as the sole modes of communication because television has transformed us into a visual generation.

Serious preaching that has as its goal the relaying of the truth of God's Word to the congregation, that is alive with the power of God, is a commodity that is all too rare today. If in certain churches the Word of God is inadequately preached, it is no coincidence that those same churches are plagued by moral decay. P. T. Forsyth was not far wrong when he declared that it is by preaching that Christianity stands or falls.

Christianity stands or falls by the preaching of the Word because Scripture is God's self-disclosure within which we hear God's law, from which we receive his promises, and by which his Christ is made known to us. Preaching is vital. It is indispensable and irreplaceable. It is the means, the only means, by which the congregation can be instructed in "the whole will of God" (Acts 20:27; also see Appendix IV, "Renewing the Worship of the Local Church").

Furthermore, there is an indissoluble unity between Word and sacrament, and together they have a powerful evangelistic impact. It is of course true that within evangelicalism both the Lord's Supper and baptism are diversely interpreted and practiced. Through this diversity different relations to the gospel are established. Nevertheless, at the very least we have in the Lord's Supper and baptism visual representations of those truths about God's grace and Christ's death that are declared in Scripture. Neither the water of baptism nor the bread and wine of the Lord's Supper is the medium of communicating God's grace. God's grace is made known in his written word and given in Christ. The Holy Spirit, who works in the presence of faith, applies the benefits of Christ's death to us. But the sacraments do point to this reality in different ways in our churches. They are, therefore, visual sermons that can be heard by unbelievers who are not participating in them.

Conclusion

The local church supports and undergirds evangelism both directly and indirectly. Its direct involvement is obvious in its gospel preaching and its related ministries, as well as in its support of missionaries and evangelistic enterprises at home and abroad. But in this chapter we have focused on the church's indirect support of evangelism because the direct connections grow out of and are nourished by the indirect.

In the Western world, the single greatest cause for diminished interest in and support for evangelism is the erosion of confidence in the uniqueness of Christian faith. Television, urban life, and the secular mentality all combine to reinforce the idea that there are many religions, many different worldviews, many different life-styles, and many different values, and that the toleration of pluralism is one of the few certainties that should be upheld in society. This combined assault has eroded Christian confidence and demolished conviction. It has made faith an exclusively private matter, something solely between the individual and God, a matter that is to be kept completely in the private domain. Christian faith is thereby cut loose from its claim to universal truthfulness and relegated merely to the domain of interior experience. Its truthfulness is thus relativized. It is true for those who choose to believe it, and it is not true for those who choose not to.

The consequences of this enculturation are not always evident because those who have allowed the culture to maneuver them psychologically still think of themselves as Christian believers who love God through Christ, believe his Word, and seek to serve him in the world. Indeed, many of these Christians do render fine service to others and are known as Christians. But insofar as they have surrendered their hold upon Christ, insofar as they no longer think of him as the necessary and unique savior of sinners, their support of evangelism will have diminished.

It is for this reason that the roles of worship and of preaching in particular have been accented. Few people find it easy to swim upstream, to be out of step with the larger crowd, to appear odd to peer group and contemporaries. In a pluralistic culture or in one where the pressures to create religious syntheses are great, those who say that Christ is uniquely true, that he alone is the way to salvation, and that those who do not believe in him are lost—these people are out of step and are, by almost any reckoning, odd. However, this experience of alienation is a distinguishing mark of biblical faith, and its absence is a telltale sign of worldliness. And worldliness is in our churches.

But worldliness dissipates like the morning mist under the power of the preached Word. The allure of worldliness—its promise of acceptability and normality in the wider culture—cannot be compared with the allure of walking with God. It is this vision that some of our evangelical churches need to rediscover. We need that renewal of the Spirit that will make biblical truth a bracing reality in our lives, Christian worship a joyful and invigorating experience, and our life in the world one of effective witness and service. Without this foundation of spiritual reality, it is not possible for evangelism to be generated or even widely supported in our churches. May we pray, then, for the renewal that we need and that the Spirit can bring!

Chapter V

Spiritual Power Encounters

Power is the ability to fulfill one's will or wishes; power is being able to bring about what one wants. In that sense, it is a game in which we all play. Power is not wrong in itself. It becomes wrong when its objectives and its results are wrong. It is not, therefore, power itself that corrupts. It is the need for power, the hunger for its exercise and for the benefits of dominance that corrupts. And this is a cruel trick we play on ourselves, for we imagine that in gaining the ability to do as we want we will find life, whereas in actual fact we exhibit only our own dying in so doing. We come to resemble overheated lovers who stoke the flames of desire with exotic aphrodisiacs only to find that these potions, far from producing unparalleled bliss, bring on irreversible impotence.

It is no surprise that the New Testament speaks of our salvation as a power encounter. For God must enter the world we have fabricated for ourselves and illumine its fraudulence. He must deal with the ego and its capacity for reconstructing reality in ways that serve its private interests, and he must sever the link with the powers of darkness whose proxy the ego is.

This divine intrusion, illumination, and liberation was adumbrated by Jesus in John 16:7-11, although as we shall see, it is developed for us principally in the epistles. The Holy Spirit, Jesus declared, would convict the world of "sin and righteousness and judgment." The title given to the Spirit here—*paraklētos*—is, as we have seen, a rich word with diverse meanings: Comforter, Counselor, Helper, Standby, Advocate, Intercessor, Strengthener. Its literal meaning is "one that is called to the side of another." It was used originally in a legal setting, and so it came to refer either to an advocate or to a prosecutor. Of the four passages in John's gospel in which it is used, three clearly use the word to mean advocate, to refer to the Holy Spirit standing by the Christian's side to aid, plead with, and encourage him or her (John 14:15-17; 14:26; 15:26). The remaining passage, John 16:7-11, uses the word to mean prosecutor. To the Christian, the Holy Spirit is an advocate (cf. 1 John 2:1); to the world, however, he is a prosecutor.

The world is completely mistaken about sin, righteousness, and judgment, and it is the Holy Spirit's work to expose the world in its folly. He will reprove it and convince it, Jesus said. Without this divine work, evangelization would everywhere be a futile undertaking.

It is one of the paradoxes of life that although the consequences of sin are experienced daily, our world understands little about sin. Every day, television news—in the West, at least, where there is a free press—is full of stories about rapes, robberies, warfare, industrial strife, deceit, and arrogance. Newspapers recount and deplore what is wrong with society. Psychologists, counselors, and ministers are regularly visited by people whose lives are in chaos and who often don't know why. In society as well as in our personal relationships we are plagued by sin, yet we have very little sense of it. Our world does not understand itself! And this ignorance poses a greater danger to human life than budget deficits, unprincipled capitalism, rampant Marxism, or proliferating weapons systems. This is so because our understanding of sin affects everything else. It is at the root of our understanding of ourselves, of what is right and wrong, of how society should govern itself, and of how nations should behave. Most fundamentally, it is at the root of our relation to God. It is the Spirit's work, therefore, to reveal what has sundered our relation to God, what destroys our relations with one another, and what has shattered our internal lives. And without this divine work, one suspects, the world would be moving swiftly toward a complete elimination of the very idea of sin.

If the world is oblivious to the nature of its sin, it is often blasé and uncaring about righteousness. In secular societies, righteousness is supposedly what results when the greatest number suffer the fewest intrusions upon their personal quests for peace and prosperity. Personal freedoms and a stable society are not inconsiderable blessings, but they have little to do with divine standards of righteousness whose presence becomes evident where the Spirit has done his exposing work. What he exposes is our vulnerability before the moral requirements of God. It is a vulnerability that links our past, present, and future. Guilt (or shame) runs it course and culminates in the judgment of God. The greater our sense of vulnerability before God's law, the greater our sense of apprehension before his judgment, and the greater will be our need for a righteousness that is not our own. Thus the Holy Spirit's work of convicting is a mighty apologetic for the atonement of Christ, for that work in which Christ took our sin as if he had committed it himself and gave to us his righteousness as if it were ours.

The Cross, therefore, is an eschatological event, because it brings forward into time a partial realization of the judgment of God. For those who stand in Christ, the judgment is already past. For them there is now no condemnation. For those who stand outside of Christ, however, the Cross is a somber and awesome revelation of God's relationship to sin and of the judgment to come.

Inasmuch as the Cross is eschatological, the world of evil forces is also judged; Jesus says so specifically in John 16:11, although the full and final sentence has not yet been carried out (cf. Rev. 20:10). It is as if two people were playing chess. At a certain point, one of the players rises from the table, leaving his opponent to ponder his next move. The opponent struggles with all the possibilities because he is determined to win. What he has not realized is that there are only a limited number of moves that he can make, and not one of them can change the outcome of the game. No matter what he does, he will lose. Just so at the Cross, the outcome of the chess game between God and Satan was decided. God will certainly win. Satan, however, is presently playing out every conceivable option, imagining that somehow his rebellion will triumph. It will not.

Thus the world, the flesh, and the devil are not invincible competitors but doomed adversaries. In his work on the Cross, Christ conquered them, and through the work of the Spirit, that conquest is brought into our modern world. It is a conquest of both truth and power, and thus our evangelization must itself be characterized by both truth and power. Men and women are not simply ignorant but are under the dominion of the world, the flesh, and the devil, and that dominion must be broken. They are not simply the pawns of alien forces but also people who have willingly believed lies about God and themselves (John 8:42-46; Rom. 1:18; 2:8; 2 Thess. 2:10-12; James 3:6); they need to know the truth as it is in Jesus.

This confrontation of truth and power does not always follow the same pattern all over the world, although the protagonists are always the same. Sometimes it is the confrontation of power that is more prominent, and sometimes it is the confrontation of truth that is more overtly significant; however, the two must always be united, for the truth of the gospel and the power of the gospel both arise from the same Jesus Christ. He is the truth and the power of God (John 14:6; 1 Cor. 5:4; 2 Cor. 12:9). It is instructive, then, to see how this confrontation works against the three forces from which we need powerful liberation: the flesh, the world, and the devil.

Liberation from the Flesh

The most basic encounter of truth and power is that which takes place in fallen human nature. Because it is so basic, because it is present in so much of what the New Testament says about the Spirit's work, we have already touched upon all of its elements. Nevertheless, we need to consider these elements again briefly in order to provide ourselves with a full perspective in which to consider the third and most dramatic of the encounters in a balanced and biblical way.

Anyone who understands the reality of the power encounter that is involved in regeneration and conversion also understands the reality of sin. Understand the one, and the other makes sense. So what does the Bible say on this matter? It assumes everywhere and asserts in several places that the state of sin is a way of being in which all participate. Pelagius was deceived in thinking that some had lived without sin. Within all of us is an inherited principle of sin from which arises a stream of sinful acts (Rom. 5:12-21; 1 John 1:8). This means that all are "under" sin, whether Jew or Gentile. Paul demonstrates what this means. It means that there "is no one righteous, not even one," that there is "no one who seeks God," that "all have turned away . . . ; there is no one who does good, not even one," and that all "fall short of the glory of God" (Rom. 3:9-12, 23).

Once, before the Fall, we had a nature that took pleasure in God's will, but this is no longer so. Now the mind is darkened to spiritual things, the will and the heart are alienated from God, and the conscience has become insensitive (cf. Rom. 5:6; Eph. 4:18-19). Fallen human nature is pitted against and implacably opposed to God's will. So deep is this opposition, so irreversible is it, that Paul asserts that fallen human nature can neither submit itself to the law nor please God (Rom. 8:7-8). Fallen human beings knowingly and wantonly give themselves to the sin in which their broken natures express themselves. This cycle and life of sin excludes the possibility of living on God's terms (cf. John 1:13; 3:5; 6:44; 8:34; 15:4-5; Rom. 7:18, 21; 1 Cor. 2:14; 2 Cor. 3:5; Eph. 2:1, 8-10; Heb. 11:6). It is a bondage that not only precipitates God's just condemnation but also betrays its bond to Satan whose rebellion it reflects (John 8:44; Acts 13:10; 1 John 3:8).

Consequently, the restoration of fallen human nature is expressed in radical language in the New Testament. There is no suggestion that this change can be made simply by rectifying a life-style or correcting some faulty thinking. The most dramatic language possible is used to describe this restitution, the required death of this sin-loving, God-defying nature and the necessary birth of a new nature by a divine, creative act (Rom. 6:1-10; 7:1-6). This exchange is a *power encounter*. It is an encounter whose miraculous nature, Paul suggests, parallels the miraculous nature of creation itself. Upon that ancient chaos, as upon the human heart, only darkness prevailed. But God issued his command that light should shine. That light, in its recreative function in human life, gives us "the knowledge of the glory of God in the face of Christ" (2 Cor. 4:6). The transformation of fallen human rebels into Christ-honoring, Christ-serving men and women requires a mighty encounter by the Spirit of God. This creative act may be invisible to the human eye and thus may lack some dramatic qualities. Nevertheless, it is at the center of everything that Christ and the apostles declare about power encounters.

Liberation from the World

The encounter between Christ and the world is far more difficult to describe than that between Christ and fallen human nature in the process of redemption. What gives the latter encounter clarity and definition is its redemptive nature. Because the New Testament describes in such detail the nature and working of sin, the work of Christ on the Cross, the way in which the Holy Spirit applies Christ's work to sinners, the agencies that he uses, and the results that one can expect, we can know in some depth what takes place in the encounter between Christ and sinners. The absence of this redemptive work in the wider society, however, means that there is no clarifying center or focus for our understanding of the ways in which Christ encounters the world.

We have already noted that the word "world" has two principal meanings in Scripture. First, it is used to refer to creation, the physical and natural world of which we are a part. Second, it is used to refer to the system and network of values in each society that are developed independent of God, his Christ and his Word, and have humankind at their center (cf. Rom. 1:25). In this sense the word indicates how fallen human beings have reconstructed life, how they have normalized their sinning. Worldliness is the extrapolation of the sinful lives of individuals in a larger cultural context. For this reason, worldliness may vary from culture to culture, because the collective expression of our sinning sometimes varies from culture to culture. But worldliness is what makes sin look normal in any given social context, and what at the same time makes righteousness appear abnormal.

As the two meanings of the word "world" indicate, Christ's relationship to the world is complex, because the created world is good whereas the world of human values is bad. The problem is that the two are usually experienced not in isolation from one another but in conjunction with one another. In the past at least, this has produced some highly aberrant attitudes in the church. Because of the goodness of creation, some have had difficulty seeing cultural perversion and have been insufficiently aware of how it has intruded even upon the church's own life. Because of the perversion of culture, others have separated themselves from the world, sometimes physically (closeting themselves in monasteries) but more often psychologically, thus losing their sense of God as creator, sustainer, and providential ruler. In so doing they have abandoned society to its own fallenness.

We need, therefore, to make a distinction between the world in Christian experience and the role of the Christian in the world. This distinction should help to illumine the different relationships we have or should have with the world, as well as the different ways in which Christ is encountered in society.

Paul links the world, the flesh, and the devil, not merely because they are related subjects but because from the viewpoint of experience they are a unity. The immediate source of sin is our own corrupted and sinful nature; the context that nurtures, validates, and normalizes that sinning is the world in whatever cultural form we find it. Thus our redemption from Satan and the kingdom of darkness requires a redemption from the guilt of sin as well as from our captivity to its bondage. This bondage is not only personal but cultural; we need to be emancipated from the power that fallen social values exert over us, for they can come to control us as the puppeteer does the puppets. It is for this reason that we are to be "in" the world but not "of" it (John 17:15-19) and why being on friendly terms with the world is always a matter of spiritual adultery (James 4:4-5). Excising, cauterizing, and destroying the influence of the world on our minds, our psyches, our perceptions, and our actions is the work of the Spirit in sanctification, and he does this work especially as we submit ourselves to the Lord (Rom. 12:1-2). We should be in no doubt about the importance of this matter. Purity of intent and action and costly commitment to biblical standards of truth and practice are the *sine qua non* of effective

Christian service. There are no other terms, no other ways of service if we choose to serve on God's terms and in his way.

The role of the Christian in the world is more complex because Christ's relationship to it is more complex. The pronouncements of Scripture concerning this role are far less explicit and thorough than its pronouncements about Christ and fallen human nature. H. Richard Niebuhr's discussion of this subject in *Christ and Culture,* though perhaps too simplistic in its solutions, has been seminal in isolating the elements in this relationship. According to Niebuhr, Christ maintains multiple relationships to culture, and so should the Christian. Sometimes the relationship is one of antithesis, sometimes one of identity, sometimes one of reformation, and sometimes one of transformation. These different relationships grow out of the fact that there is both good and bad in human life, and often the good and the bad are experienced together, perhaps even simultaneously. In some instances what is wrong is so evil that it can only be opposed (antithesis); sometimes what is wrong can be eliminated in order to secure the possibility of something much better (reformation); at other times what is mediocre or ineffective can be changed into something truly beneficial (transformation); and sometimes elements are good in themselves and need only to be confirmed and defended (identity). Christians can probably find instances of all of these relationships in their societies, and in all of them the truth of Christ must be made known. For this witness, this exercise of responsibility is the context, the accompaniment that gives credibility to the preaching of the gospel. Perhaps two illustrations will suffice to show how these different relationships to the world come into play in Christian involvement in society.

First, consider the issues raised in large urban settings. Large cities everywhere raise special difficulties for evangelism because they are the breeding ground of pluralism. Different worldviews, religions, ethnic interests, and life-styles are brought into close proximity with one another. If strife and conflict are to be avoided, the competition among these worldviews, religions, and so forth has to be contained. This usually occurs in two ways. First of all, in most large cities there is a geographical separation of ethnic, tribal, or religious groups. In many North American cities—such as Boston and Chicago, for example—the history of the city can be traced simply by discovering its pattern of ethnic growth. In Chicago there are areas that are predominantly Polish, Irish, Chinese, Puerto Rican, and Vietnamese, and these areas coincide with the growth the city underwent during periods of mass immigration. The physical separation of these national groups not only minimizes conflict but also allows for the preservation of the cultural, social, religious, and linguistic customs of these people. But such separation is not the total solution, because considerable contact across these boundaries occurs in the work-place. Here is where the psychological solution to conflict comes into play: all cultures, religions, and languages are granted equal legitimacy. This psychological acceptance, however, is only a step away from allow-ing that all religions are not only lawfully legitimate but equally true. That step is easy to take where secularism is as pervasive as it is in North America. The result, then, is relativism and pluralism.

In contexts of oppression this situation develops a different dynamic. Because economic exploitation and violence become endemic, criminal conduct becomes normalized. This in turn wreaks havoc in the com-munity. It produces habitual suspicion on the part of those who are most oppressed. This suspicion creates a siege mentality that may be impene-trable. Among those who somehow gain power, be it economic or politi-cal, it produces icy indifference and a capacity for inhumanity. Among those without power, it produces fear, hopelessness, and a fatal indif-ference to the issues of life. In this context, how should evangelism be undertaken?

The message of Christ needs to be projected in three ways. First, it needs to be made clear that Christ's messengers have no worldly al-liances; for example, they cannot allow themselves to be co-opted by the interests of colonial rule in Africa or of any indigenous nationalism. They bring a message whose values are different from the values espoused by those with worldly ambition, and this brings them into conflict with all forms of oppression. This element of antithesis needs to be stated wher-ever possible. Not only so, but active and positive measures need to be taken to reform the situation. This reform is often practical—simply meeting basic human needs for food and clothing, for example. Second, the gospel of Christ's forgiveness must be stated unambiguously. Re-sponding to social need is not the gospel. It is not a substitute for or an alternative to the gospel. Salvation comes only through believing in Christ, who died in the place of sinners, bearing in their place God's righteous condemnation, and thus effecting reconciliation between God and sinful human beings. Third, the alternative community of the church needs to be established in order to provide a living example of how people can relate to one another in terms of Christ's values. In South Africa, for example, a converted Afrikaner should find in the church a community that desires to accept men and women of all races because Christ has accepted men and women of all races. This discovery should raise some deep questions about those laws enacted by the government that not only prohibit this acceptance but also produce inhuman conditions for many blacks. Likewise, a converted black businessman who has shamelessly exploited fellow blacks in his township should find in the church a concern for and estimation of others that simply disallows this exploitation. The recovery of a biblical perspective is what the church should nurture and require. Thus the church should oppose what is evil (antithesis), undertake constructive action to meet basic human needs (reformation), and seek to strengthen the significance of the image of God (identity).

A second example of how Christ's relationships to the world come into play in Christian involvement in society is found in the nest of issues raised by the emergence of the "information society," especially in the industrialized West. In such a society, interpersonal relationships are different from those in the past because of the movement from mass media to "mini-media" and thence to personalized media. The development of miniaturized equipment and the expanded capacity for the transfer and storage of images and information, coupled with the breakthroughs of satellites, cable stations, and computers, are changing the nature of communication and consequently changing the way people see the world.

We cannot say with certainty what path the proliferation of information and of information systems will take. But we can already see one possible pattern in the emerging centralization and concentration of information that enables large multinational corporations to dominate the media, broadcasting their message to millions. Likewise, there is a growing internationalization as TV programming crosses cultural and national boundaries. The potential for profit in this new access to consumers has hardly passed unnoticed, so there is a massive commercialization of the airwaves. At the same time, there is an increasing diversification, particularly through cable networks and VCRs, of programming and consumer choice: viewers can watch news, sports, sitcoms, movies, or other forms of entertainment at any time they choose. The impact of these changes can be predicted with reasonable accuracy. It will create a global, electronic village dominated by big business and show business where the aim is to say less and less to more and more people. This will lead to media imperialism on the one hand, and on the other, to passive, self-absorbed, introverted viewers, people who can easily be manipulated and whose skills in personal relations, whose capacity for community and fellowship, will shrivel.

Regardless of whether this is precisely the shape that the "information society" will take, media will always communicate reality in the same way. Electronic media succeed because they are able to make us think that we are a part of the action. This is the great potential the media have, and it is the great danger they always pose. This illusion of participation occurs within a reality that is shaped in particular by television. It has the potential to create a pseudo-environment, and the resultant danger is that viewers may then judge all of life in the light of this false perception. Because it creates the illusion of participation in problems and events, it also leads us to confusing *doing* something with simply *knowing* something about a problem. As the influence of the media grows, the greater will be the tendency to see the world through media spectacles. As the media bombardment grows, so too will the danger of information overload, the result of which is that viewers increasingly act as if they are narcotized.

Television not only creates a pseudo-environment; it also changes reality by selecting and filtering what it shows us. If television is our window on the world—and it is—then we need to remember that it functions just as a window does by giving a selective view. What we perceive to be "out there" through television is only what a producer has decided should be seen on the screen.

This point is especially important when we consider the values that are transmitted, values which, like the images that communicate them, are carefully selected and can easily be confused with what is actually "out there." The Western media indoctrinate viewers with a number of foundational values. The media teach that the survival of the fittest is important, and hence programs stress the importance of exercising power over others and over nature; that happiness consists in material acquisition, and thus programs frequently feature "the good life" with all of its symbols of affluence like designer clothes, powerboats, Ferraris, palatial residences, and vacation homes in the Bahamas; that each person needs to actualize himself or herself, and thus programs suggest that what is pleasant for the individual is ethically good, regardless of whether this involves sexual promiscuity or violence; and that progress is inherently good, and hence most programs are cut loose from the past, are disdainful of history, and assume, without ever quite saying it, that a brand-new civilization is in the making.

What, then, should the church be saying and doing as the "information society" takes shape? First, the church should point out that an inversion of values has taken place: people should not exist for the media, but the media should exist for people. In the scramble for wealth and power that the media offer to those who own and use them, it is people who have been abused. Often people are important to media moguls only because they can be fleeced and used. Second, the church should point out that the specific values being transmitted in slick, appealing forms are often injurious to human well-being. These points need to be made by Christians within the media; they need to be made by voluntary organizations who assume the responsibility of bringing pressure to bear on the sponsors of particularly offensive programs (in contexts where television is not state-run) through organized boycotts of their products. And churches need to educate Christians about the deleterious effects that television may produce. In these ways the relationship of Christ to culture is one of antithesis.

But television does not have an intrinsic moral bias. It is a medium that can be used for good or ill. Christian use of television, however, is not simply a matter of broadcasting sermons or Christian talk shows. According to George Galiup, who has taken polls about the effect of TV in America, non-Christians cite Christian television as creating the largest impediment to believing the Christian gospel. There appear to be several reasons for this. First, too many practitioners of Christian television have run afoul of the law in terms of their personal finances and taxes. Second, too many give the impression—despite protestations to the contrary—that one of the marks of the good life is an abundance of material possessions. The third problem is one that non-Christians do not cite, and it has less to do with the practitioners than with the viewers. In North America there are literally millions who "go to church" only in front of their television sets. While they may receive some teaching as they would in church, many other vital elements are missing. The TV "pastor" does not know his flock, despite the illusion of personal communication that TV creates; there is no community, and there are no personal relationships; there are no opportunities for service; there is no administration of the Lord's Supper; and there is no discipline. Indeed, the only demand that is made upon the viewer is financial.

What changes should be made in Christian television? Perhaps it might become possible for Christian television at least to move away from broadcasting to "narrowcasting." Within local areas, what is communicated through the media could easily be related to and tied into local churches. This change would help solve the abuses of accountability on the part of some television preachers, and it would make the message more personal than that delivered by "national" pastors. It would encourage local participation in television, and in that way it would begin to work at making television serve the people rather than be served by them. There are already examples of these changes in Christian television, and they show how this aspect of the world can be transformed for Christ. Thus in television there is at least the possibility for both antithesis and transformation.

In relating Christ to culture, then, what is foremost is the way in which we relate his truth to our culture. The operation of his power in providence is often mysterious. Of course, Christ is sovereign, and therefore he has "determined the times set for them [all nations] and the exact places where they should live" (Acts 17:26). He has established the boundaries for each nation and each civilization; he raises one up and puts another down. This can and must be affirmed, but the ways in which Christ exercises his divine power vary and are not always clear to us. Nevertheless, Christ's truth must be brought to bear upon the world. While it is the Holy Spirit's function to do this, we should remember that he works primarily through the exercise of Christian responsibility in antithesis, reformation, transformation, and identity.

Liberation from the Devil

It is in the sphere of religion that we are most likely to encounter demonic power, for it is in this sphere that people choose to submit themselves to a higher power. In the secular West, demonic power is usually veiled and deceptive, but in societies where there is an easy acceptance of the supernatural, it is naked and unashamed. Indeed, certain occurrences today are reminiscent of those in the Gospels and the early church.

In most non-Christian religions there is a rational element, and it was for this reason that the first chapter of this book ended with a call for apologetic work. Often, however, there is also a nakedly demonic element operative in these religions, and for this reason we need to see Christ's power, his conquest on the Cross, realized in an evangelistic context.

Jesus called Satan "the prince of this world" (John 12:31; 14:30; 16:11). John warned that the whole world is "under the control of the evil one" (1 John 5:19). Paul also took this theme of cosmic warfare seriously. Those who are dead in sin, he said, are also in bondage to "the ruler of the kingdom of the air" (Eph. 2:2); unbelievers are blinded by "the god of this age" (2 Cor. 4:4). But Paul's most frequent metaphor for these satanic forces is "rulers and authorities" (Rom. 8:38; 1 Cor. 15:24, 26; Eph. 1:21; 3:10; 6:12; Col. 1:16; 2:10, 15). The argument that "rulers and authorities" refers to worldly values and institutionalized evil simply cannot be sustained exegetically. While it is true that worldly rulers may serve the cause of evil, may even be demon-possessed, and that laws and social patterns may normalize evil and demand loyalty to that wickedness, the rulers and authorities that Paul refers to in his correspondence are satanic forces.

Christ's Work as Liberation

It is therefore important to observe that both Jesus and the apostles set the Cross in the context of a confrontation of power with these evil forces. To be sure, this is not the only interpretive motif in the New Testament; as a matter of fact, it is not even the central one. Nevertheless, it is present and needs to be understood alongside and integrated with the other New Testament themes.

What is most significant about the development of this theme is that it is never treated in isolation from the others. Undoubtedly, Satan exercises his control over the world, but this control is not one of mere raw power; rather, it is a control that must be exercised through our love for and allegiance to sinning. Only in extreme cases does this love and allegiance grow into a complete dominance and possession of the sinner by demons. Thus, when the New Testament speaks of liberation, it does have Satan's dominance in mind, but it emphasizes the means to break that dominance.

Redemption language that is used to describe Christ's death is also used to describe the release of prisoners of war by the payment of a price. Release and payment are separate but inseparable sides of the same act. From what, then, are we being released? From a combination of sin (Rom. 6:11), the curse of the moral law (Rom. 7:9; Gal. 3:13; Col. 2:14), and the requirements of the ceremonial law (Gal. 4:4-5). Thus Christ has liberated us from the guilt of sin (Rom. 3:24; Eph. 1:7; Col. 1:14; Heb. 9:15) and is presently liberating us progressively from the power of sin (Titus 2:14; 1 Pet. 1:18). What is the basis for our release? Christ's offering himself as a ransom (Mark 10:45; Titus 2:14), giving himself in our place, dying for us when we should have died (Acts 20:28; Eph. 1:7). He secured our liberation from sin and death by himself paying our price, standing in our stead, bearing in our place the wrath of God. It is in this way that Satan's control is severed, because his control is through sin. It is in this way that Satan's realm is plundered, because his is a realm of wickedness. The translation from the kingdom of darkness to that of light is a translation from Satan's world to Christ's kingdom. It is a divine, glorious, and irreversible liberation. And for that reason, Paul boldly declares that, "having disarmed the powers and authorities, he [Christ] made a public spectacle of them, triumphing over them by the cross" (Col. 2:15).

From a biblical perspective, then, liberation from Satan is a part of the gospel proclamation. How that bondage is experienced, of course, varies greatly from culture to culture. In Africa, there is great fear of the spirits, and the gospel is heard, perhaps even primarily, as the good news of deliverance from these spirits and the fears they provoke. In Indonesia and Brazil, there is evidence of powerful occult undercurrents with overt demonic activity. In Brazil today it is reported that sixty percent of the population has engaged in witchcraft, voodoo, and other practices of the occult. Likewise, in Hindu cultures there is a pervasive fear of the spirit world. Sometimes whole families have spells cast on them, and believers who find deliverance through Christ nevertheless have to struggle with the aftermath of these entanglements—sometimes for years after their conversion. In the West, secular people dismiss the supernatural with casual indifference, but at the same time, they are often astonishingly credulous about astrology. Although occult practices are also gaining in popularity, the main bondage most Westerners experience is still the desire for affluence. Westerners have allowed the pursuit of "the good life" to shape their perspective, values, and psychology as profoundly as Africans have allowed their fear of spirits to shape them. The gospel promises liberation from all these forms of bondage. To be sure, it promises liberation from that most basic of all bondage—to sin and its consequences—but Christ's death secures not only a right relationship with God but also freedom from the fraudulent values of the world and the tyranny of Satan's hosts.

It is this last point that has provoked considerable discussion in recent years. Along with the promises of forgiveness that the gospel holds forth, should we also expect to see demonstrations of divine power that both validate that gospel and visibly exhibit the liberation from Satan's tyranny? Should we look for and expect "signs and wonders" as an accompaniment to the preaching of the gospel? In order to provide a framework in which to explore the different options, we need to trace this theme in the Scriptures and then pursue it in the early church.

Signs and Wonders

Early Developments

It is often said that in the Old Testament there is no Hebrew word for "miracle," but this is not true. There are in fact a variety of words roughly corresponding to the Latin *miraculum*, from which the English "miracle" is of course derived. Three such words are *niflā'ôt*, *môfet*, and *pelā'ôt*, roughly corresponding to "wonders" (the first two) and "signs" (the last). It is true that the Old Testament, with its direct and theistic approach, did not divide phenomena into "natural" and "supernatural," as we do. Both modes of operation were alike seen as the work of God. Nevertheless, the Old Testament recognized that at certain times and for certain reasons, God was pleased to act "wonderfully"—that is, in a way that made his activity obvious by the unusual nature or scale of the event. God sometimes did this as a "sign" to encourage faith or to convince doubters. The same event could therefore be both a "sign" and a "wonder." From either aspect, the value of the event was that it was uncommon. Usually God worked in what we properly call "normal" ways, although they were equally God's work to those who had eyes to see. The Psalms, for instance, see God constantly at work in nature (Ps. 65:9-13); the Prophets see God's hand in every event of history, unspectacular and spectacular alike.

It should also be remembered that such "signs and wonders" are not scattered uniformly throughout Israel's history. Judging from the evidence of the Bible, they occurred in "clusters," presumably during strategic periods of God's revelation to Israel, either because of particular dangers or because a new period was beginning. The Exodus period is one such epoch; the days of Elijah and Elisha, another; the times of Daniel, a third; and the days of the Gospels and Acts, a fourth. All this can be statistically established. There are, of course, other instances of signs recorded between these "peaks," but they are isolated and usually occurred for very special purposes (e.g., Hezekiah's healing and the sign of the sundial; 2 Kings 20:7-11). Therefore, while "signs and wonders" are an integral part of God's self-revelation, they are not a continuous part of it. To put it bluntly, they are the exception, not the rule, over time. Indeed, it is this very feature that gives them their value; if they were constantly occurring, they would mean little.

Further, it should be noted that spurious "signs" and "miracles" are known in both the Old Testament and the New. Pharaoh's magicians could produce wonders too (Exod. 7:11), although at the last they were defeated (Exod. 8:18; 9:11). The Old Testament is full of magicians, necromancers, and the like (e.g., 1 Sam. 28:7), and it never makes the modern mistake of denying them any power; it simply denies them ultimate power and forbids Israel to have anything to do with them (e.g., Lev. 19:31). That is why the deepest proof of the genuineness of an Old Testament prophet was not merely his working of wonders or his foretelling of the future (Deut. 28:22) but the nature of his "word"—whether or not it was in conformity with God's revelation (Deut. 13:2-5). This "test" was both highly significant and very profound; it revealed the "false prophets." In the Old Testament false prophets consistently appear alongside true prophets; indeed, in later days there were far more of them. They had powers, but the immediate source of those powers were in question. Thus the Old Testament shows that "miracles" in themselves may be misleading and are therefore of limited value.

We find the same attitude toward miracles in the New Testament, where the two words *sēmeion* and *teras* are used for "sign" and "wonder." The word *dunamis,* meaning "act of power," is also used. Jesus himself warned that false Christs and false prophets would arise and perform signs and wonders that would deceive many into thinking that their claims were genuine (Mark 13:22). We are prone to think that the "reality" of the "miracle" is in question, but, while this may well be the emphasis in isolated cases (the Bible certainly tells of such frauds), most of the time it is not at issue. It is not the reality of the miracle but the source that is in question.

It is precisely because false prophets can do these remarkable things that many will be deceived by them. This adds point to the bitter accusation by "the teachers of the law" that Christ expelled demons through Beelzebub (Mark 3:22). The teachers were correct in recognizing that the enemy could work miracles as well as God (see Rev. 13:13-14). They were hopelessly wrong in their assumption that the enemy would use this power against himself (Mark 3:23).

But let us return to the beginning of the Gospels. The coming of God's Son into the world (itself a miracle and "a sign"; Luke 2:12) heralded a unique burst of miraculous activity, as was only to be expected at such a time. Christ performed miracles (Mark 1:32-34); even his foes admitted that (John 11:47). True, he refused to give a "sign" to unbelievers (Mark 8:12), but he did so because "signs" in themselves would never convince such people (Luke 16:31), although, rightly viewed, they can lead to faith (John 20:31).

Jesus gave his apostles the power to heal and to expel demons as well as to preach (Mark 6:13). There is no doubt that this exercise of a "miraculous" ministry was an immense help to the proclamation of the gospel as well as a visible sign of the coming of the Kingdom. But at times it also seems to have been a distinct hindrance to the preaching ministry of Christ—why else did he often move away when the crowds demanding healing became very large (Mark 1:38)? Perhaps it was partly because such crowds left him no time to preach; they came to Jesus to experience miracles (John 6:26).

Thus we already have at least four motives for the sparing use of miracles even in the New Testament. First, in themselves they denote power, but not necessarily divine power. The disciples performed miracles, but so did the false prophets. Further, although the disciples always performed miracles in the name of Jesus (Mark 9:39), some of their opponents did too. The sons of Sceva, for example, performed miracles "in the name of Jesus whom Paul preaches," although they were taught a rough lesson because they themselves had no personal knowledge of that Jesus (Acts 19:13-16). Second, miracles may divert attention from the "good news" of Jesus, which alone truly leads to spiritual salvation. Third, miracles may be selfishly sought simply for the recipients' benefit (to satisfy curiosity or to meet some physical need), without sufficient consideration of spiritual goals. Fourth, miracles may be regarded simply as "magic" (extraordinary events that have no relationship to the God of the Bible), a common concept and apparently a common experience, at least in the pagan world of the first century. The well-known story of Simon of Samaria shows what a real danger this was (Acts 8:18-19).

But the fact still remains that, whenever the Old Testament prophets looked forward to the messianic age, they described it as an age of miracles. The deaf were to hear, the dumb were to speak, the blind were to see, the lame were to walk (Isa. 35:5-6). It is also clear that this messianic age dawned with the coming of Jesus; miracles were thus not incidental to his ministry but integral to it, although (as noted) not necessarily universal. In his "programmatic sermon" in the synagogue of Nazareth (Luke 4:16-22), Christ read the passage from Isaiah (61:1-2) that foretold the coming of one who, blessed by the Spirit, would perform miracles, and Christ claimed that he was the fulfillment of that Scripture. No one doubts that physical miracles were also pictures of the spiritual miracles worked by Christ, but that is not the point here. They were certainly physical miracles as well, and important in their own right.

Jesus specifically committed powers of healing and exorcising to the Twelve (Mark 3:14; 6:13); there is no evidence that a wider group of people possessed such powers at this time, which seemed to be the case after the Day of Pentecost. That the Twelve exercised these powers is clear from their own reports. The occasional failure, honestly chronicled in Scripture (Mark 9:18), only underlines the expectation of general success. However, it is only fair to point out that no version of the Great Commission links a promise of "signs and wonders" to the preaching of the gospel, with the exception of the later ending of Mark (16:17-18), which is probably inauthentic. In other places, the preaching of the gospel and its spiritual results are mentioned alone (e.g., Matt. 28:18-20).

When the Day of Pentecost came, not only was there a general manifestation of "tongues" (Acts 2:4)—the exact form of the manifestation is not important and therefore need not detain us—but Peter readily claimed that this was the messianic "age of wonders" foretold in the Old Testament (Acts 2:16-21). This was confirmed by the healing of the lame man at the temple gate by Peter and John (Acts 3:6-7); we can see from the context that this miracle was an impressive illustration of and a powerful "drawing card" for the gospel. It is reported that the apostles performed many "wonders and miraculous signs" (Acts 2:43); it is also reported that Stephen performed "great wonders and miraculous signs" before his martyrdom (Acts 6:8). Paul clearly performed many miracles of healing (Acts 19:11-12), including at least one instance of raising someone from the dead (Acts 20:10). Nevertheless, we must note that we do not know how widespread such gifts were among early believers. All that Acts allows us to say with certainty is that the apostles themselves undoubtedly possessed these gifts and used them (cf. Acts 9:32-41).

In the Epistles, however, it appears that, while some "ordinary" Christians did possess these gifts (1 Cor. 12:28-30), instances of their use were more rare. Was this because most evangelism in the early days was done by "apostolic men," who already had the gifts, rather than by the "ordinary" Christians? That seems unlikely. Were these gifts peculiarly connected with evangelism or independent of it? Whatever the explanation, it is an observable fact that the world of the Epistles was in many ways different from the world of Acts. This is all the more surprising because at least the earlier Epistles must cover the same time period as the later section of Acts does. Nevertheless, it is only fair to say that the miraculous, for whatever reason, occupies a less significant place in the Epistles than it does in Acts. This is said advisedly, because in the later chapters of Acts miracles are mentioned less frequently and are therefore less emphasized than in the earlier chapters. The point should not be pressed too far. Miracles did occur frequently in the earlier life of Paul, as the later chapters of Acts record (the blinding of Elymas in Acts 13, the healing of the lame man in Acts 14, the exorcism of Acts 16, the deliverance from jail in the same chapter, the Ephesian healings in Acts 19, the raising from the dead in Acts 20), just as miracles figured in the reports of Barnabas and Paul to the Jerusalem church (Acts 15:12). Nevertheless, miracles were not constantly occurring as before. In Paul's later career, miracles occurred less frequently. Indeed, from chapter 20 until the end of Acts, there are few references to any miracles. Apart from God's providential care of Paul (e.g., 27:43) and Paul's prophetic knowledge of that care (27:22-26), the only other instances to note are those in which God preserves Paul from snakebite (28:5) and heals Publius's father (28:8)—apparently the prelude to a general campaign of healing on the island of Malta (28:9). Whether or not Paul performed miracles at Rome, we do not know; there is no biblical evidence one way or the other.

When we come to the Pauline epistles, there are surprisingly few references to miracles in any form, whether exorcism, healing, or otherwise. It is clear that "healing" (1 Cor. 12:9) and "miraculous powers" (1 Cor. 12:10) are numbered among the gifts of the Spirit, and therefore it is equally clear that, like speaking in tongues (1 Cor. 12:10), these gifts were in evidence, but the very terminology used seems to make plain that they were not universalized gifts (1 Cor. 12:7-11). In the letters to the Galatians, the granting of these gifts is mentioned only incidentally (3:5), so perhaps they were in evidence but taken for granted in Galatia. This may have been the case elsewhere too, which would explain the few explicit references to these gifts in the text. Romans 12:6-8 does not mention them at all.

And nowhere in the Epistles is the performing of miracles ever commanded either as an adjunct to or as preparation for preaching the gospel. This silence is important to our understanding of the relation between evangelism and the miraculous. True, James enjoins the healing of the sick by the anointing of oil and praying (James 5:14), but this is a matter-of-fact instruction about church members given to the elders of the early church. No evangelistic associations accompany it, nor is it seen as a specific "sign," whether for unbelievers or believers.

Later Developments

In the patristic period, spiritual gifts, particularly "signs and wonders," were neither possessed by many nor exercised regularly. By the opening years of the third century, these gifts appeared to be waning. And apparently they were not manifest consistently or uniformly throughout the church.

Nevertheless, the early fathers did see the church as a charismatic community inasmuch as it was within this community that the Spirit's gifts were manifest. Irenaeus provides one example. In a striking statement he described the Christians' exercise of the Spirit's gifts:

> Those who are in truth His disciples, receiving grace from Him, do in His name perform [miracles], so as to promote the welfare of other men, according to the gift which each one has received from Him. For some do certainly and truly drive out devils, so that those who have thus been cleansed from evil spirits both believe [in Christ], and join themselves to the Church. Others have foreknowledge of things to come: they see visions, and utter prophecies. Others still, heal the sick by laying their hands upon them, and they are made whole. Yea, moreover, as I have said, the dead even have been raised up, and remained among us for many years. And what shall I more say? It is not possible to name the number of the gifts which the Church throughout the whole world has received from God, in the name of Jesus Christ . . . and which she exerts day by day for the benefit of the Gentiles.

Of these gifts of the Spirit, two were especially prominent in the patristic period: prophecy and exorcism.

In the middle of the second century, prophecy was a common occurrence in Christian congregations. The emergence of the Montanist movement, with its aberrant interest in prophecy, in no way changed this. True, the critics of the movement opposed the Montanists' exercise of prophecy. These critics charged that the Montanist prophets had lost their humility and unwisely identified themselves with the Spirit in their moments of ecstasy. In addition, the Montanists claimed that only those who granted Montanist effusions the status of revelation were true Christians. But, although these claims and practices greatly offended non-Montanists, the acceptance of the gift itself was not diminished. Indeed, one of the Montanist critics charged that there was too little prophecy in Montanist circles. Christ had promised that prophecy would be an enduring gift, this critic pointed out, and no new prophets had arisen among the Montanists. "They could not name anyone," he said, "even if now fourteen

years have passed since the death of Maximilla." During the first half of
the third century, however, it appears that the gift of prophecy died out
more or less completely.

The same could not be said of the second major gift, exorcism, which
the fathers believed was given to every Christian. It enjoyed unrivaled
prominence. The reason is easy to see. The other gifts such as prophecy,
glossolalia, and healing all had their parallels and imitations in pagan
cults and religions; exorcism had no such parallel. In exorcism a confrontation
took place between Christ and all of his supernatural contestants
and rivals. As a result, Christians were seen to be not merely exponents of
"new magic" but servants of the living God. A statement by Tertullian
illustrates the point:

> Let a person be brought before your tribunals, who is plainly under
> demonical possession. The wicked spirit, bidden to speak by a follower of
> Christ, will as readily make the truthful confession that he is a demon, as
> elsewhere he has falsely asserted that he is a god. . . . . What clearer than a
> work like that? What more trustworthy than such a proof? The simplicity of
> truth is thus set forth; its own worth sustains it; no ground remains for the
> least suspicion. Do you say that it is done by magic or some trick of that
> sort? You will not say anything of the sort, if you have been allowed the use
> of your ears and eyes. For what argument can you bring against a thing that
> is exhibited to the eye in its naked reality? If, on the one hand, they are
> really gods, why do they pretend to be demons? Is it from fear of us? In that
> case your divinity is put in subjection to Christians. . . . . If, on the other
> hand, they are demons or angels, why . . . do they presume to set them-
> selves forth as acting the part of gods?

When confronted with a Christian who commands them in the name of
Christ, the demons are forced to speak not only the truth about themselves
but also the truth about who Christ is and where he is now positioned: he
is God's Son, reigning at the right hand of God.

When the church was engaged in direct confrontation with paganism,
exorcism amounted to a practical proof of Christ's superiority over all the
"gods" of the pagans. "It has not been an unusual thing," Tertullian said,
"for those testimonies of your 'deities' [in exorcism] to convert men to
Christianity, for in giving full belief to them, we are led to believe in
Christ."

In the patristic church, demon possession was invariably regarded as a
Gentile phenomenon and was associated with demon worship. Before
catechumens were baptized, several exorcisms were pronounced in order

to free them from any demonic possession. And even if they were not demon-possessed in the strict sense of the term, they were nevertheless regarded as polluted because of their participation in demon worship. According to the Epistle of Barnabas, their hearts were seen to be "houses of demons":

> Before we believed in God the habitation of our heart was corrupt and weak, like a temple really built with hands, because it was full of idolatry, and was the house of demons through doing things which were contrary to God. . . . When we received the remission of sins, and put our hope on the Name, we became new, being created again from the beginning; wherefore God truly dwells in us, in the habitation which we are. How? His word of faith, the calling of His promise, the wisdom of the ordinances, the commands of the teaching, Himself prophesying in us, Himself dwelling in us. . . . This is a spiritual temple being built for the Lord.

In the earlier fathers, then, there was a natural congruity between the church as the habitation of the Spirit and the church as the instrument of the Spirit's power. The same Spirit who had created the world also created the church in union with Christ; the same Spirit who had imparted life to God's people also bestowed upon them supernatural gifts whose exercise would exhibit the power and truth of God, even in confrontation with the powers of darkness.

It is now difficult to avoid the conclusion that patristic faith and practice anticipated in significant ways what has taken place in today's charismatic movement. The wheel of church life seems to have completed a full revolution, although it has taken centuries to do so.

Underlying this statement are three assumptions. First, this statement assumes that the charismatic movement has already transcended the earlier Pentecostalism to which it has at least been allied if not joined. This is clear from the fact that the charismatic experience is not tied into a Wesleyan doctrine of perfection, as was early Pentecostalism, and from the fact that speaking in tongues is not always seen as the necessary validation of the Spirit's infilling. The change is also evident in ecclesiastical settings where charismatics flourish, settings that would have dumbfounded earlier Pentecostals.

Second, linking the early patristic church and the charismatic movement assumes that there is nothing historically unique about the charismatic experience in the twentieth century. Charismatics—and perhaps, more commonly, Pentecostals—have often argued to the contrary. It is true that today the presence of the Spirit's gifts are universal in a way that they were not in the second century. But the comparison is misleading because Christianity itself is universal today in a way that it was not in the second century. If this is borne in mind, the argument for the uniqueness of today's charismatic phenomenon seems to fall apart.

Third, seeing similarities between patristic faith and practice and charismatic faith and practice assumes that contemporary charismatic phenomena have no self-evident eschatological significance. If there is a reason for thinking that these phenomena are the realization of the prophet's prediction of the "latter rains," that reason seems to lie not so much in the biblical text as it does in the assumption that today's charismatic movement is historically unique. If that assumption is questionable, then so too is its eschatological counterpart.

The conclusions drawn from the similarities between the early patristic period and the current situation in our churches will vary with the interpreter. Some will see this parallel as indicating that we are moving back toward a more superstitious faith; others will argue that it is a movement toward a more biblical faith; still others will add that all that has transpired between the second and the late nineteenth centuries is in varying degrees inadequate, erroneous, or apostate. The one conclusion that can be safely drawn is that the cyclical nature of church life, which can be demonstrated in many areas, is a solemn reminder of how easily the fullness of Christian life is lost, and that the goal to which all need to strive is finding the combination of a full-orbed and uncompromised biblical orthodoxy, fearless and consistent biblical practice, and winsome, authentic spirituality. We cannot choose to have theology apart from spirituality, or spirituality apart from theology. And we cannot choose to have personal piety apart from social piety, or social piety apart from personal piety. The Bible calls for the kind of wholeness that embraces all of these elements.

The Contemporary Debate

The contemporary debate about spiritual gifts is, of course, wider than the question in focus here. Our concern is to ask whether it is right to expect "signs and wonders" to accompany the preaching of the gospel. Are these predictable concomitants to the fullness of the Spirit? Alternatively, were they concomitants only to the apostolic office and role, and hence did they cease with the cessation of that office and role? Or are they periodically realized in the life of the church and thus not predictable concomitants but nevertheless possibilities to be realized when and as the Holy Spirit sees fit? All three positions have been argued.

The first position—that exorcisms and miracles, especially healing, should always accompany evangelism—is usually based on three major presuppositions. First, the argument draws heavily on Kingdom motifs and in particular on the image of the gospel as a weapon in the strife. The preaching of the gospel places the evangelist on the cutting edge of the contest between Christ and Satan. This conflict is one of power as well as truth, and the exercise of this power is seen to lie both in personal deliverance from guilt and sin and in external expressions of that power of Christ's Cross in deliverance from Satan or from bodily sickness. Second, this position assumes the continuance of the nine gifts of 1 Corinthians 12:8-10, and the exercise of healing is often linked with one or more of the other gifts. Third, this position assumes that the coming of the Holy Spirit at Pentecost inaugurated a new age of miracles that is without parallel because the Holy Spirit's coming in this way is without precedent. The unprecedented nature of this bestowal, it is argued, is clearly seen in the Book of Acts, which offers a set of case studies in which the link between miracles and evangelism is presented. There are references to four miracles, not counting Christ's appearance to Paul (Acts 5:1-11; 8:39; 13:11; 28:3-10), seven references to healings or exorcisms (Acts 3:1; 5:15; 9:1-18; 9:32-35; 14:8-10; 16:16-18; 28:3-10), and six references to signs and wonders (Acts 2:43; 5:12; 6:8; 8:6; 14:1-7; 19:11, cf. 13:11). In addition, strange phenomena in nature (Acts 16:25-26) and angelic visits (Acts 8:26; 12:8) are recorded. That these events revealed the great, outpoured power of the Spirit is beyond dispute. So, too, in the manifold response to the preached Word was the Holy Spirit's mighty convicting power revealed. It is true that direct associations between miracles and belief are scarcer. Nevertheless, such a link can be seen in Acts 9:32-35 (the healing of Aeneas and the conversion of many in Lydda and Sharon), in Acts 13:6-12 (the blinding of Elymas and the proconsul's conversion), and in Acts 16:25-34 (the earthquake and the conversion of the Philippian jailor).

The second position on signs and wonders is built upon two main presuppositions. The first presupposition is that the appearance of miracles in the Bible is rhythmic and that their appearance was concentrated at those times when fresh revelation was being inaugurated. The second presupposition is that the inauguration of the fresh revelation of the New Testament was an apostolic responsibility that ended with the conclusion of the apostolic ministries. For this reason healings are no longer needed, for their real purpose was to authenticate the apostolic authority in opening God's Kingdom to Jews and Gentiles alike. Today the gospel is authenticated by the Spirit but unaccompanied by outward miraculous manifestations.

The third view of signs and wonders accepts the notion that miracles in the Bible appear according to a rhythm but questions whether the connection with the apostolic office can be established in so airtight a manner.

How, then, should we think about miracles? We should begin by realizing that the manifestations of the miraculous in the Book of Acts do not represent a spiritual plateau. Nowhere in the New Testament is there even a hint that this reduction of manifestations corresponds to a lowering of spiritual temperature, a common modern explanation of this phenomenon. While the New Testament prophesies a coming spiritual declension (2 Pet. 3:3) and even points to it as already present in some instances, there is no hint that the Christian church as a whole was any less "spiritual" at that time than in the early days of Acts. After all, the episodes involving Judas, Ananias and Sapphira, and Simon of Samaria all occurred in the early days, when the New Testament constantly records that the church was filled by the Spirit (Acts 4:31; 5:12-16). Nor did this "aura" preserve even the leaders from occasional error or sin (Peter, Gal. 2:11; Barnabas, Gal. 2:13). Thus it seems more biblically accurate to see the "rise and ebb" of spiritual manifestations as something controlled by God's purposes rather than as a reflection of the "rise and ebb" of spiritual life.

This also helps to explain why God often (but not always) gives such manifestations to simple folk in the early days of gospel preaching and church planting in missionary areas, especially if (as usually happens) these people are fiercely opposed or even persecuted by those of the existing faiths. The same holds true for simple Christians today who face persecution in totalitarian states. At such times, "signs and wonders" have a clear evidential value, but their presence or absence seems to depend more upon the needs of the local church than on the person, spirituality, or ability of the gospel preacher.

There is, however, one other aspect that is very obvious to any missionary working in such circumstances, and no doubt it was equally obvious to the first-century missionaries. Similar "signs and wonders" occur—speaking in tongues, healings, and the like—in all the other religions of the world. Outwardly considered as phenomena, they appear to be indistinguishable from those miracles connected with Christianity. It will not do to say that those signs and wonders of other religions are "bogus" while those of Christianity alone are "genuine." In terms of physical effect there is often no difference between them, although the source of their spiritual power is very different. Some would explain this by saying that God wishes for healing for all his creation, and in his mercy he acts through other religions to effect such healing, even outside the realm of full revelation in Christ. The unbelieving and materialistic West, which has ruled out the supernatural in advance, will explain all such miracles in terms of "psychosomatic" factors or the influence of mind over matter; some might call them "faith healings," irrespective of what or who the object of faith may be. These are important views to consider, but they are not vital for the present argument. The important thing for us to note is that such "miracles," although they occur, are not done in the name of Jesus but in the name of of some other god or religion (even if that religion be only Western materialism). They are therefore utterly apart from the gospel and in no way assist its furtherance. They are thus another illustration of the fact that "signs and wonders" in themselves do not advance the gospel; only when they are done in the name of Jesus do they have evangelistic value. Presumably, this was the thought in John's mind when he cautioned us not to trust all spirits but to test them to see whether they come from God (1 John 4:1). He explained this by saying that there are many "false prophets" who presumably can produce mis-leading signs. He noted that a useful test involves determining if these spirits clearly testify to the incarnate Jesus (1 John 4:2). If a "sign or wonder" does not do this, it is at best a "dumb sign" and at worst a misleading one (see Acts 14:8-18). In itself, therefore, the actual miracle is not important; it is what it signifies and from whom it comes that is important.

Perhaps the last word should be allowed to come from Paul, who was, as we have seen, both a mighty evangelist and a mighty miracle-worker in the plan and purpose of God. In 1 Corinthians 12, Paul lists spiritual gifts like miracles, healing, and speaking in tongues along with prophecy and teaching. He has carefully shown that not everybody has each of these gifts (vv. 29-30), even though he acknowledges their importance in the last verse of the chapter (v. 31). Yet in the very next verse—the first verse of 1 Corinthians 13—Paul tells of a gift far better and greater than all of these: the gift of love. It is this short chapter more than any other passage in the whole New Testament that helps us keep our sense of perspective. We must not be blinded by the more spectacular gifts, because they are limited in their effect. Only love is unlimited (1 Cor. 13:8, 13).

Conclusion

However we choose to resolve the question of "signs and wonders," and regardless of what our particular view of the Spirit's gifts may be, we should all be clear on the Spirit's mission in the world. In *the most basic of all power encounters,* he brings life and light to fallen sinners whose rebellion has produced only death and darkness. In a mighty creative act, he produces that new nature which alone can love God and serve Christ. In the wider society, the Holy Spirit strengthens and makes effective Christian witness in ethical protest, in loving service to those on the fringes of society, and in the appropriation of cultural vehicles for Christian truth. In specific contexts, we may be brought face to face with overt demonic activity and its consequences. It is by the Holy Spirit that Christ's conquest over sin, death, and the devil at the Cross is realized in our own time, thus showing us again the "incomparable riches of [God's] grace, expressed in his kindness to us in Christ Jesus," for God has "raised us up with Christ and seated us with him in the heavenly realms" (Eph. 2:7, 6).

Chapter VI

Spirit of the Living God, Fall Afresh on Us

It is nineteen centuries since the Holy Spirit fell upon the beleaguered disciples at Pentecost. They were probably as amazed at the results as we are today when we read about them. Despite our familiarity with the story, we can still project ourselves back in time and take our place in that crowd. We hear again the great apostolic preaching, we see the awe, we feel the coming of that power like a tidal wave sweeping all before it. We are in the midst of the scenes of sorrow, weeping, and anguish. And we also see those believing, rejoicing, and glorifying God. If only our times were like theirs, we think wistfully to ourselves. Today we face humdrum faith, joyless churches, and fallow, ineffective evangelism. Have we lost this divine power forever? Can we ever expect that the Holy Spirit will show the same mighty working again?

In the late twentieth century we often become obsessed with these questions. What seems to impress us most about the Book of Acts is how the disciples got the job done—unlike our churches, which seem to fail at the task. They got results and we do not. Belief today is threatened by unbelief, by the cold indifference of secular culture and the competition and belligerence of other faiths. What often strikes us about Christian faith today is its impotence; what amazes us about the early believers is their power! They were accused of turning the world upside down; we are dismissed as irrelevant.

We think to ourselves that perhaps, lying unnoticed in the Book of Acts, is their secret of success, a secret that somehow did not get passed along with the faith. So begins our earnest search through the pages of Luke's narrative for the missing formula. And when we find it, we think, we too will be catapulted into noisy scenes of repentance, weeping, joy, and the glorifying of God. Perhaps our church will even have to launch a building program to accommodate all the new growth. Better still, it might have to seek new and *much* larger premises! These visions of success dance in our heads like medieval angels, thousands of them. There seems to be no limit to how many can play together in our minds. But on Sunday, the church is the same, the organ is as choked and off-key as always, the singing is as joyless as ever, the sermon is as flat as last week's, and we are again left wondering whether we have missed something vital in the Book of Acts.

The working of the Holy Spirit is undoubtedly mysterious, and we have to admit that we do not always know why God's unusual blessing falls on some people rather than others, on some ages rather than others. At the same time, however, his working is never random. We know in principle what the work of the Holy Spirit is, and we know in general the kind of people whom he is pleased to use in the extension of Christ's Kingdom.

But what we know in principle and in general collides head on with the obsessions that all too frequently drive us to search for the formula of success in the Book of Acts. We search the pages of this book not primarily because we want to learn about God's will and his ways but because we want to be successful. The desire to see men and women come to Christ is biblical; the need to be successful is not.

Success is the sacrament of a secular age. Its outward and visible signs are affluence, prestige, power, the ascent of the corporate ladder, the wider influence, the bigger church, the biggest audience. Its inward and invisible grace is its sense of having arrived, of being somebody—somebody who counts, somebody with clout, somebody who has to be reckoned with. To be successful is to enter the new, secular age; it is to be saved. There are pastors who want to be successful, and when they long for the growth of their church they are also longing for the blessings and accoutrements of success. There are Christian leaders who want, almost more than anything else, to be somebody. Somebody who is known, who has power. Somebody to be reckoned with. Somebody who is successful.

This motivation in the search for God's power is especially noticeable in societies where succeeding is important; in contrast, the search for God's power in the Bible is inseparable from suffering, humiliation, and the loss of those things that give us standing in the world. It is not for nothing that Jesus spoke of the disciple's cross, of losing limbs and eyes, of the hostility of the world (not its acceptance and adulation) that would have to be borne. So where have we gone so wrong?

The answer is implicit in these pages. We have here encountered the Holy Spirit in his three major functions: he exhibits the truth, he engenders holiness, and he exercises divine power. These functions are also characteristics, for what he does expresses who he is. And the simple point that has to be rediscovered and should never have been lost is that the Spirit's power comes only in conjunction with his work of truth and holiness. Our obsession with his power is really an obsession with results. At its basest level, it is an admission that we will solicit converts on almost any terms and that gospel preaching can legitimately be carried on by almost anyone, regardless of how he or she lives. In thus seeking naked results we are dividing the Spirit's work of power from his work of truth (with respect to the convert) and of holiness (with respect to the evangelist). We are dividing what cannot be and is not divided. The Holy Spirit's work of power is powerful precisely because it is a work of truth and of holiness. It is power unleashed in conviction about sin, righteousness, and judgment; it is power exhibited in the new life of the believer. It is never power naked and raw, power unrelated to Christ, power unrelated to the demands and character of God, power that is promiscuous and aimless. Power of this kind bears more resemblance to that of Satan than to that of the Holy Spirit. Thus it is the relationship between the Spirit's power and his work of truth and holiness that now needs to be explored further.

Truth and the Spirit's Power

The New Testament is actually remarkably circumspect in describing many of the Holy Spirit's works because it focuses on Christ and his Cross. Although the cosmological role of the Spirit can be inferred from—and, indeed, is required by—the full Trinitarian understanding of God that the Bible contains, the New Testament explicitly limits what it says about the Spirit. After the Incarnation, the Spirit's link with Christ's work becomes unmistakable and indissolvable. He is Christ's Spirit, the Spirit of God's Son, whose work is dependent upon, grows out of, and is defined by that of the Son.

This relationship can, of course, be developed in two entirely different ways. Those theologies that have cut "the Christ" loose from the historical Jesus—that do not identify the one with the other and therefore do not think of "the Christ" in terms of the words and acts of Jesus—have also cut Christian faith loose from Christian particularism. They can speak in terms of the "cosmic Christ." They can equate this Christ with a universal Spirit. They are able to see a divine presence in all human spirituality, regardless of what religious form it takes. It therefore becomes a matter of simple charity to acknowledge that among devout Hindus and Buddhists no less than among ethical atheists there are "anonymous Christians." This approach is expressed in slightly different ways, depending on whether the proponents are Roman Catholic or Protestant. Nevertheless, the search for a universal spirituality is the same on both sides of the theological divide, as is the price that has to be paid to secure it.

The alternative is to identify the historic Jesus with the risen Christ— the only alternative that the New Testament allows. The work of the Spirit, then, is that work which brings to realization in the lives of men and women what Christ secured for them on the Cross.

In this context, truth is not merely what is valuable, beneficial, and profound to the person; it is what is valuable, beneficial, and profound in the person and work of Christ. The Spirit illumines our minds to understand the Scriptures, and through the truth of the Scriptures he thus glorifies Christ.

The consequence of this for evangelism is clear. Evangelism may involve explanation and persuasion, but it must be explanation and persuasion relative to Christ. Biblical conversion is conversion that is brought about by *truth*. The gospel is not merely a way to ease pangs of guilt or to recover lost self-esteem. It is what brings about an encounter between truth and unrighteousness, between Christ and sinners. It aims not merely at changing the attitudes of sinners but at convincing sinful men and women to surrender their right to themselves, acknowledge their sin, lay hold of Christ's death for them, turn from the path of rebellion, and trust in the grace of God alone for their redemption. It is this gospel, this interest in truth, this concern for the centrality and indispensability of Christ and his death that the Holy Spirit blesses. This is a deep and profound gospel because it is a gospel of truth, not simply one about behavior modification or attitudinal change. Do we want to know the Spirit's power? Do we want to know the apostles' secret in the Book of Acts? Their secret was this gospel of truth, and their experience was that the Spirit of truth used its faithful proclamation to secure the conversions of thousands of people. It is a secret that is open and public, a secret that should be ours.

Holiness and the Spirit's Power

Ours will be remembered as a time in which our private and public lives were sundered from one another. At least this is true where urbanization has been a force shaping society. Cities are centers for manufacture and commerce that develop their own environments, both psychologically and ethically. This environment, as well as the physical distances traveled to and from the workplace, means that many of us live in two different worlds, the personal and the public. All too often, each world has its own values, and far too few people know how to resolve the competition between these worlds.

Gone are the days when people knew their cobbler and their grocer personally, when services and goods were offered on the strength of personal reputation, when character included both one's personal and public life. Today, who knows who is responsible for shoddy and defective workmanship? Assembly lines are anonymous. This anonymity shapes much of our public life, and it produces a diminished sense of responsibility. We do, say, and think things in our public, impersonal lives that we would question or deny in our private, responsible lives. This is as true of corporate executives as it is of assembly-line workers. For example, it is not unknown for a businessman to behave like a faithful and attentive husband at home and to pursue an affair with his secretary at work. At home he upholds the values of honesty and hard work when talking to his children, but at work he engages in corporate tax evasion and dishonest business practices. At home he is generous and caring, but at work he is rapacious and callous. He suppresses the conflict between these worlds, the tension between these contradictory lives, so that neither set of values ever becomes completely dominant. This man remains an ethical hybrid.

For the Christian leader, of course, this situation is reversed. His or her public role is not anonymous but highly personalized and visible. This man or woman is a model and therefore has to be seen expressing Christian values. To occupy such a role, he or she has to be seen to believe the right things (theology), to care about God and his truth (piety), and to be appropriately indignant about the depravity in society (ethics). The private role, however, is out of the spotlight, and it is here that the fracturing of life often becomes evident. We know of too many Christian leaders who have filled the public role admirably, who have been towering strengths of orthodoxy, perhaps evangelists with significant followings and leaders in various crusades against social evils, but whose inner lives have slowly crumbled away. Some married leaders have become entangled with other women; more have gone through divorces; some have had extravagant tastes; others have suffered the deterioration of character over time, the harsh notes of pride and domination all but eliminating the soft and beautiful strains of humility and self-abnegation that may have been there in the beginning. Our world makes this kind of breakdown seem almost inevitable because we have come to accept the idea that our private and our public lives are essentially different. If such breakdown is inevitable, then it seems as if it might also be pardonable.

But that pardon which we extend so easily and even with a sense of piety is a depth charge whose detonation demolishes the biblical teaching on holiness and spirituality. In accepting what should in fact be repudiated and even exposed, we are setting ourselves completely at odds with the work of the Holy Spirit. Can we continue to be baffled, then, that we do not experience his powerful blessing in our lives and on our ministries?

It is one of the ironies of modern evangelicalism that while it has upheld the biblical doctrine of sin, it has largely succeeded in eliminating the biblical doctrine of worldliness. Three decades ago, in many parts of the Western world, evangelicals believed that worldliness meant indulging in smoking, drinking, dancing, and attending movies; today these taboos have largely fallen away, at least in private practice. That they are no longer the focus of prohibition is not altogether wrong. It may be that smoking, drinking, dancing, and movie attendance are sins, but if so, they are minor sins compared with others encompassed by the biblical understanding of worldliness. Embracing the world and its value system is a scarlet sin; going to a movie usually is not. But what has supplanted the old taboos? Have they been replaced by a deeper sense of what worldliness means? The answer, all too often, is that the taboos have been replaced by no sense of worldliness at all.

In biblical terms, the world is that system of values whose source is human sinfulness and whose expression is cultural. It is that collective life which validates our personal sin. It is everything in society that makes sinful attitudes and practices look normal. Worldliness is the "cool" life, what encourages us to think, for example, that different sexual life-styles should be accepted as part of our pluralism, that personal gratification is a right, and that self-interest expressed in career, material acquisition, and power is the goal to which all of life's processes should be directed and, where necessary, bent.

Worldliness is also what allows us to accept as unavoidable, and even as normal, the bifurcation of life into its public and private spheres. It is what allows us to pass over flagrant sin in the one sphere or the other as if it were unimportant. It is what makes us the enemies of God.

The biblical norm is so clear and simple that its restatement sounds almost banal. That holiness which the Holy Spirit produces, which is the consequence of union with Christ, includes and encompasses both the public and the private spheres. It is what binds together private attitudes and public work, the interior and the exterior, our relationship to God and our relationship to others, our attitude about ourselves and the exercise of our responsibility in society. Holiness is not contained within or limited to any one of these aspects; it belongs to them all. Holiness is expressed in our theology and our piety as well as in our ethics; that is why the New Testament treats heresy as a moral rather than an intellectual problem. Holiness in the church is that corporate expression of our union in Christ which gives us a community of support for what is right and which acts as a counterweight to that worldly community which favors what is wrong. Holiness in society is the expression of all those values of the Kingdom that call into question the normality of sin and that already are beginning to realize the conditions of the "age to come."

Our world easily creates a fissure between our identity and our witness; those who are under its influence therefore imagine that Christian witness can float free of Christian identity, that what we say can be dissociated from who we are. Evangelism is thereby seen as a process that is unrelated to the moral life of the evangelist. Evangelism is thought to be biblical merely if it states what is true. But this is only half the truth. To be the biblical gospel, evangelism must be true, but it must also emerge from a context of personal authenticity in the evangelist, for the Spirit who is the Spirit of truth is also the Spirit of holiness. He cares about the lives of those who witness to Christ even as he cares about what they say. Christian identity and Christian witness are integrated with one another, just as our behavior in the world is associated with the impact that we can expect the gospel to have on that world.

Evangelism is not simply the transmission of information. It is not a form of advertising. After all, who knows and who really cares about the lives of those who advertise products on television? Only where these electronic merchants have the glare of publicity focused upon their lives for some reason and only where this publicity generates negative feelings in the public is their capacity to sell put in jeopardy. The disengagement of character and product is usually the norm. It is a norm that may also

have suggested a model for the Christian church, but it is a model supplied not by Scripture but by the world. The biblical model is quite
different. Those who "declare the praises" of God (witness) are those
who have first been called "out of darkness into his wonderful light," who
have become "a people belonging to God" (identity). Without the reality
of this transformation in status and existence, their declaration has no
substance (1 Pet. 2:9-12). Thus the gospel has a clear context: on the one
side are the people who are called out and have become "a royal priest-
hood," a "chosen nation," and on the other are those who are under the
domination of the world, the flesh, and the devil, and who have yet to
believe. Peter goes on to tell us that non-Christians will be moved by the
truth of this gospel when they see the moral integrity it inspires in the lives
of Christians who avoid "sinful desires" and do "good deeds." Indeed,
this is the model we also see in Acts 2:42-47. This young Christian
community exhibited its love for God in teaching, fellowship, worship,
and prayer, and showed its love for others in caring for the needy. When it
lived out its identity in vibrant obedience, its witness was mightily effective, and the Lord added converts to its community daily. This is, in fact,
the model that is everywhere evident in the New Testament. It is there in
specific teaching and in tacit assumption; it is found in the first churches,
and it is modeled in the first apostolic witness. It is there as an underlying
demand. It is there as an unavoidable responsibility. Yet somehow we
have succeeded in avoiding it.

The call of God the Holy Spirit, therefore, is for men and women who
will be people of character and integrity, those whose public and private
lives will be governed by the same moral norms, lives that together will
reveal the transforming life of Christ. It is a call for those who have the
character to live this kind of life in the midst of our fallen world, in the
process expressing both God's truth and his holiness. It is a call for those
who will so witness to Christ that what they say will be undergirded by
truth and righteousness, and thus the gospel will take on that awesome
authenticity which is its power. The Holy Spirit is the Spirit of truth and
holiness. Where he finds men and women who are people of truth and
holiness, he has those whose ministry and witness can be powerfully
blessed. We ask for his power today.

We therefore join with those across the ages who have learned that it is
God alone who gives power to the gospel, reality to faith, and effectiveness to human witness. He is his own evangelist in our evangelism. It is
our evangelism that must be enkindled by his presence in it, and among
us.

Come, Holy Spirit, heavenly Dove,
    With all Thy quickening powers;
Kindle a flame of sacred love
    In these cold hearts of ours.

Come, Holy Spirit, heavenly Dove,
    With all Thy quickening powers;
Come, shed abroad a Savior's love,
    And that shall kindle ours.

Appendix I

The Spread of Christianity in China Today

Alan Cole

One of the most remarkable Christian phenomena of the past few decades has been the rapid growth of the Christian church in China. While exact figures are in dispute, the fact of growth is undoubted. According to rough estimates, there were a million Protestant Christians in China at the time when all foreign missionaries were forced to withdraw by the newly established Communist government. Today, according to the most conservative estimate, there are at least four million; verification comes from both government statistics and official church figures. It is hard to say how many Christians there are outside the organized church. Exaggerated estimates of twenty million or more should probably be rejected, but my own observation has convinced me that there are probably three or four Christians outside the organized churches for every one in them. Whatever the exact figure may be, the point is that there has been a large increase in the number of Christians.

The second point to make is that the majority of these new converts were won to Christ during the worst years of the so-called Red Guard and Cultural Revolution, a time when terrible persecution overtook not only the Christian church (both organized and unorganized) but everything that smacked of the old order. Growth at such a time will not surprise church historians who agree with the early church father who said, "The blood of the martyrs is the seed of the Church." But it is still remarkable that such growth has taken place before our very eyes in a totalitarian society that is committed by dogma to oppose the Christian faith and, indeed, all religious beliefs. We may still need to ponder how this growth has occurred, even if there is no longer a question as to why it has occurred.

The third point is that, if my observation is correct, much of the growth has taken place in villages and communes among very simple peasant people. It is true that congregations and groups have also reappeared in most if not all of the cities and big towns, but much of this seems to be a reassembling of "faithful remnants" of the old congregations, with the addition of many younger people converted through their witness. This is of course equally wonderful, but if I am not mistaken, the burgeoning of faith in the country areas is the real "growing edge" of the Christian church in China today. The Communists have their own explanation of why growth occurs in the country. They point out the supposed superstition and ignorance of the peasants, and their sense of helplessness when faced with unmanageable natural disasters like storms and floods and earthquakes, coupled with their lack of understanding of chance, "natural causation," and scientific principles. These factors, the Communists say, predispose country people to accept Christianity. But why should these factors make them more likely to accept Christianity than to return to Buddhism or older and more familiar Chinese religious folk beliefs like Taoism? There has been some return to Buddhism, it is true, but it has occurred on a much more limited scale and (from my observation of a few temples, if these are typical) mainly involves the very old and the very young—not the large section of young to early middle-aged people that is found entering the Christian church. Further, this return to Buddhism seems to be only a nostalgic turning back to the old, not an adoption of a new faith. There may be new converts to Buddhism in Western lands today; I have heard of none such in China.

Can we draw these three points together to explain the way in which Christianity has spread so rapidly in China during these years? Is there any other factor that accounts for the growth? Of course, the faithful witness of countless ordinary Christians, by life and word, has been central. Wherever such Christians were sent—to prison, to labor camps or "banishment areas" (like Tsinghai province in the west of China), or to the depths of the country—they, like the disciples of Acts 8:4, "preached the word." And we should not forget the prayer of Acts 4:29-30, which asks for boldness to preach the word, and asks that God confirm his word by healings and other signs. This appears to have happened in many of the country areas of China (as it certainly has in rural Nepal), at least in the days of initial evangelism, but we shall return to this topic later.

Certain factors can be ruled out as significantly contributing to this rapid spread of Christian faith. First, we should note that the circulation of Christian literature has not been a potent factor, because for much of the period in question such literature was not available. There was in fact widespread destruction of Bibles and other Christian literature during the days of the Red Guard, and there were no Scriptures or Christian tracts on hand to circulate. Any such that survived were treasured by those who already were Christians, and were used (either by individuals or small groups) for spiritual nurture, not outreach. Second, while gospel radio broadcasts beamed into China from overseas were not insignificant and undoubtedly led to some conversions (as can be seen from the many letters the stations received), they do not seem to have been the major factor in church growth in the country, although they may well have been a major factor in the building up of believers.

At this point I can only state what many Christians in China have constantly told me, and in view of their known moral probity, I see no reason to disbelieve them. (By the very nature of the case, I have no direct observation or experience to report.) My sources are individuals within the organized church and an equal number of those who, for whatever reasons, are outside it. The sober report of these Christians is that, in many places, some remarkable instances of healing in the name of Christ have led people—sometimes whole families, sometimes even small villages—to turn to Christ. This conversion was not usually caused by multiple simultaneous healings but rather by one outstanding instance of healing. Nor was this initial healing necessarily followed by a sequence of such healings; if it was, my informants were either ignorant of it or did not think it worth mentioning.

A second clearly attested factor was what we may call visions or manifestations. In several instances, figures were reported to be standing guard outside the homes of Christians, deterring would-be attackers. Again, I simply report these cases without passing judgment. This is of course a familiar claim of Chinese Christianity; such reports have occurred regularly in times of persecution at least since the time of the Boxer Rebellion. But the very fact that such reports have been made repeatedly for a century suggests that they should not be lightly dismissed. After all, there are many similar instances recorded in both the Old and the New Testament. Further, had the alleged appearances been clearly modeled on the biblical stories, they would have been rightly suspect, but many bear no such resemblance. For example, the figures that Chinese Christians reported seeing were by no means always young men dressed in white, as is often the case in the Bible, nor did they always display obviously supernatural characteristics. It was just that their presence could not be explained on natural grounds or by natural causes. In addition, in the small places in the country, where everybody is well-known locally, these appearances were not comforting, as fabrications of such incidents are; they created disquiet and often fear. I shall not pass judgment on whether or not the figures were angels, but the resultant deliverance is undoubted. On one occasion, the trial of a Christian landlord, a pair of white doves appeared, fluttering about the courtroom and around the accused. They may well have been quite ordinary white doves, but why did they appear at the trial of a Christian and not at the trial of others? (Similar stories in a garbled form seem to have circulated about the martyrdom of Polycarp in the second century.) In any event, the Communist judge was sufficiently impressed by the doves to commute the usual statutory death sentence to a sentence of hard labor. He may also have been influenced by the testimony of many tenants about the behavior of this Christian landlord in comparison with that of other landlords, but it was the doves that convinced the crowds.

There are many other stories of remarkable preservations of the lives of Christians, ranging from what we might call "miracles of timing" to the story of the Christian in a North China prison who was stripped naked one harsh winter day and thrown out into the prison courtyard with the gibe "See if your God can keep you warm." God must have done so, for the man is alive and witnessing today; he says, with some humor, that he has never suffered from a cold since that time. True, there are similar stories in the early church, some ending in martyrdom and some in deliverance, but these simple Chinese Christians can hardly have heard of them. Besides, there are as many known instances in which Chinese Christians, like the martyrs of Hebrews 11:35, were delivered through death, not from it, by the hope of the Resurrection. Such preservations thus seem to have been unusual, and certainly not universal.

What are we to make of all this? On some occasions (but by no means every one), an initial work of healing led to conversion, but there is no evidence of a universal, ongoing succession of such acts. There may have been further instances of healing, but if so, none of the informants thought them significant enough to report. On some occasions, God's servants were delivered from death by either supernatural or at least remarkable means; on other occasions, they were not delivered. In these accounts I cannot trace any correlation between the healings and the belief or nonbelief of the participants. It seems that in some cases God was pleased to act so, while in other cases he was not. This would be a hopeless enigma were it not exactly the picture that we find in the pages of the New Testament. Thus, whatever the ultimate theological vindication of these occurrences, they show that God is perfectly consistent in his dealings with the church down through the ages.

How can these accounts be explained, and why are there not an equal number of reports of such remarkable events from the cities, where the church has long been established? (If there were such occurrences, I heard little or nothing of them.) I can offer only tentative explanations that may be invalid. I am reasonably sure of the facts, but not necessarily of the interpretation. I can therefore only conclude that God often graciously vouchsafes such manifestations to witness to non-Christians—especially simple people—about the truth and power of the gospel, especially in the initial stages of its presentation. Without some such "signs," these people would not be disposed to believe at all. Even so, the response is not universal or automatic; all are impressed, but only some actually believe as a result of the manifestations. Further (as is sometimes the case in the mountains and isolated regions of Nepal, where such instances are chronicled), the new believers' faith may still be very imperfect: it is at first only a faith in Christ as a healer or protector, not a faith in Christ as the Savior from sins. At this stage, these newly won hardly ever think of the Cross. At most, they think of Christ as the victor over Satan—but then, this was a favorite view in the early church too.

Perhaps this kind of response explains why (*pace* those who believe differently) the Lord himself seems to have used healings selectively if not sparingly: he did not wish to be known and followed as a mere healer any more than he wanted to be made king as a mere bread-giver (John 6:15). Nothing else can explain his steady withdrawal from areas where crowds were flocking to him for healing (Luke 4:42). Healing may have been a sign, but it was not the heart of Christ's mission, which was to preach the Good News. True, he came in fulfillment of the Old Testament promise—to heal the sick and to set the prisoners free (Luke 4:18)—but he did not deliver John the Baptist from prison and death (Mark 6:27), and Paul's "thorn in the flesh" remained (2 Cor. 12:7), as did Timothy's weak stomach (1 Tim. 5:23). This corresponds to the "progression of faith" in the Old Testament—the gradual movement from the early faith, which saw health, wealth, and long life as virtually the prerogatives of God's people, to the deeper level of faith in later days, expressed in Daniel 3:17-18: "If we are thrown into the blazing furnace, the God we serve is able to save us from it, and he will rescue us from your hand, O king. But even if he does not, we want you to know, O king, that we will not serve your gods. . . ." This deeper faith also leads to the "Though he slay me, yet will I hope in him" of Job 13:15, and the defiant "Though the fig tree does not bud . . ." of Habakkuk 3:17. Here is a faith in God that is not dependent on outward signs at all; whether God is pleased to give signs or to withhold them, the faith remains the same. This is, after all, the faith of Christ at Gethsemane: "My Father, if it is possible, may this cup be taken from me. Yet not as I will, but as you will" (Matt. 26:39).

Is it this maturity of faith (not any supposed intellectual sophistication of the city Christian that the country Christian lacks) that leads to the comparative lack of miraculous instances today among the Chinese Christians of the larger established centers? Is the miraculous the spark that ignites faith for some, rather than the steady diet by which faith is nurtured? Is it the case that, just as marriage requires more than the fireworks of the honeymoon, so Christian faith cannot thrive on an exclusive diet of the spectacular? Perhaps these are conclusions to which we cannot give categorical assent or denial, but certainly they seem to me to be the conclusions pointed to by both the biblical evidence and the present-day experience of the church in China. Indeed, although I have chosen the present-day church in China as an illustration, all that I have said here would apply equally to some areas of Nepal and East Africa, and to Muslim evangelism generally. In each a general principle is in operation.

Appendix II

The Spirit and People Groups: God's Power and Human Imagination

Alan Cole

The task of this essay is to consider if the movement of the Spirit, discernible in many parts of the world today, is linked with the "homogeneous unit principle" (the theory that churches made up of people with the same ethnic, social, and cultural backgrounds grow fastest), and, if it is, to what degree. I shall choose as a topical illustration the spiritual movement currently taking place among the aboriginal peoples of North Australia. One could also choose the current renewal movement in Singapore (largely restricted to nonvernacular churches), the present thrust for evangelism in China, or the phenomenon of "student churches" in Asia. Whether the title of this piece is altogether fair to the subject is a good question; in many cases, spiritual results seem to have come by an instinctive rather than an imaginative approach. But this may simply correspond to the difference between unsophisticated and sophisticated Christians: the former tend to operate unselfconsciously and therefore nonanalytically. However, if we believe in the guidance of the Spirit, there is no need for us to "intellectualize" every situation in a Western fashion. Instinctive Christian action in these areas can be proof of the Spirit's guidance just as much as Christian reflection on past experience.

The aboriginal work in North Australia had the attention of godly, prayerful missionaries for some seventy years, with comparatively little result. This is not to say that there were not many professions of faith and baptisms, but there was little enthusiasm for evangelism and no candidates offering to take the Christian ministry to their own people in any form. Furthermore, Christian women, apart from what they did in immediate family circles, contributed little to church life, as is culturally the pattern. About five years ago, however, a spiritual revival began on Elcho Island, an aboriginal homeland off the north coast of Arnhem Land in North Australia. It is probably fair to say that it was sparked by the visit of some charismatic white preachers from further south, but it rapidly took on a fully aboriginal flavor. I think all would agree that the movement is the fruit of the years of patient labor and earnest prayers, and a real work of the Spirit.

The movement has certain distinctive characteristics. Neither speaking in tongues nor prophecy holds a prominent place, if any at all; healing certainly plays a part, though not as a test of the Spirit's presence. In many ways the movement resembles the East African Revival of a generation ago rather than more recent Western manifestations of renewal. Much singing (especially of choruses) is typical, as are simple testimonies (often of deliverance from alcohol and immorality), simple exhortation rather than biblical exposition, and outdoor "fellowship meetings," usually held in the evenings and often lasting far into the night, especially if held at residential "Bible camps." Above all, the aborigines involved feel an urge to evangelize other aboriginal people, a task usually undertaken by groups or teams and involving simple guitar music and much singing. Out of this has arisen a new urge to minister in local groups, a desire that has produced candidates put forward by local churches rather than chosen from the outside. Christian women have played a new part in all of this. In some places, aboriginal motifs, music, and customs have become part of the movement; in others, these influences are not equally discernible, but the movement is still palpably one and the same, and moves freely from one type of group to the other. It is now spreading rapidly through the still "tribalized" aboriginal groups of the northern, western, and central parts of the country, with at least some impact on the less tribalized groups of the northeast, and no appreciable impact as yet on the totally detribalized aborigines of the big southern cities.

However, it is important to realize that this movement did not arise when vernacular languages and cultural symbols were first used in the preaching of the gospel and the building of the church. Missionary work in the north of Australia had indeed come full circle in the century of its life: at first it promoted assimilation to the Caucasian's language and life-style, then integration, then diversification. Before the recent aboriginal movement, most if not all church groups were already evangelizing and worshiping in local languages, and some had woven a considerable amount of aboriginal culture into their worship. In the latter, the Roman Catholic Church was probably the leader, with the Protestant "Uniting Church" a close second. Everywhere, old "mission stations" had already become autonomous, self-governing aboriginal townships. While these developments may have paved the way for the revival movement, they did not in themselves create it. They only created conditions congenial to its growth.

It is also important to note that a sense of unity between the many scattered groups of aborigines had been steadily growing before the movement took hold. There is no doubt that changes in government policy over the past decades have helped to foster this unity. In a professedly pluralistic and multicultural society, the aboriginal peoples, while not encouraged to separate themselves from others, are certainly encouraged by the government to treasure their language, identity, and cultural heritage. In addition, federal legislation granting aboriginal land rights has undoubtedly fostered a general sense of aboriginal unity.

In short, these factors were virtually creating a "homogeneous unit," or rather, creating the perception of one where there had been no such perception before.

Granted all these conditions, how did the spiritual movement develop? It began in one fully tribalized area and spread, with remarkable rapidity, to other similarly tribalized areas within Arnhem Land, usually by the visit of an aboriginal team of witnesses coming from a place already touched. This kind of evangelizing was not the result of any careful intellectual calculation on the part of aboriginal Christians. It simply seemed to them to be the most natural thing to do, since there already was a nascent sense of unity and even, in some cases, family relationships linking different areas. However, since almost all of these small groups speak different (and sometimes quite unrelated) languages, there was not the link of a common language. Consequently, most of the witnessing was done in English, at times verging on "Kriol," a typical local variation of Creole-type language with vocabulary derived from English but following aboriginal structures. Despite the language differences, common skin color (the movement hardly affected lighter-colored part-aboriginals further south), common traditions and culture, and common circumstances bound the groups together. It is possible that another link below the surface was the totemic system common to all aboriginal tribes, which may have increased this sense of unity and therefore helped the spread of the movement. According to this system, aboriginals who share the same totems are considered to be related, even if they belong to different tribes and language groups (e.g., the desert aboriginals and those on the seacoast). However, the force of this factor is hard to evaluate, as it is rarely mentioned nowadays, especially by Christians.

The spiritual movement so generated proved itself capable of traveling across vast distances that could be measured in thousands of kilometers: it traveled from Arnhem Land in North Australia, to the Kimberleys in West Australia, to the Queensland Coast on the east, to the tribes of the Simpson Desert in the south, sometimes passing over vast and largely "Caucasian" areas in between. This progression was, of course, no magic; it occurred simply because the revival-bearers contacted their peers (if not their siblings) wherever they knew them to be, irrespective of the distance separating them. It is no more remarkable than, say, the evangelization of a group of widely scattered Pacific islands.

The pattern that developed in each place was remarkably similar, perhaps because each place imitated the pattern brought by the team of revival-bearers. It seems likely that this pattern was brought by the revival-bearers because it had already, in the place of its origin, proved acceptable to aboriginal culture. Once again, however, it should be stressed that at this stage the introduction of such a pattern was completely unselfconscious on the part of the bringers; it was simply the form in which the new spiritual life had come to them. Nor was it claimed that the pattern was perfect or should be lasting. Indeed, it had certain grave deficiencies, notably a lack of any form of solid biblical teaching. In fact, a current problem is that the "Elcho Island pattern" tends to be followed rigidly.

The leaping over the "sea" between the "islands" was interesting if not deliberate. It is true that aboriginal Christians touched by the revival did in fact witness to Caucasians (police officers, for example, and others) who happened to be living in their settlements. To the best of my knowledge, however, they did not attempt to have any impact on purely or even largely Caucasian communities, except in those instances in which they witnessed to small enclaves of aboriginal folk living among Caucasians. This may have occurred simply because the aboriginal Christians were convinced that the Caucasians would not listen to them, and past experience would certainly support such a view. However, an equally significant factor may have been the lack of any existing cultural affinity between the two groups.

This last factor could also account for the fact that the movement has had little impact on the big "mixed" towns and cities, as distinct from the smaller aboriginal townships or "camps." The more urbanized the group of aboriginals, the less their sense of kinship with the more tribalized peoples. An extreme case are the detribalized part-aboriginals of the southern cities. Some of them wish to be assimilated into the Caucasian majority; if they are to be reached, therefore, it must be through local Caucasian churches. Others still have a strong sense of their aboriginal roots. But all of them are puzzling to the still tribalized aboriginals of the north, Christian or no. These southern city-dwellers may claim to be aboriginal, but to northern eyes they have lost land, language, culture, and identity. As one northerner said to me, "They do not know their tribe; they do not know their country" (i.e., their ancestral homeland). The tribalized aborigines have little to say to the city dwellers (on the matter of land rights, for example), not because they want it that way but because they have so little in common with the detribalized aborigines. So far this appears to have been sadly and equally true of the revival movement. If it is to involve the detribalized aborigines (as one hopes and prays that it will), it must be through deliberate "translation" by the aborigines themselves.

It should also be noted that the immediate product of this movement has been not only a typical form of evangelism but also a typical form of ministry, one suited to aboriginal communities in that it is a shared ministry, with candidates put forward by the Christian congregation (not selected on a volunteer basis)—candidates who are not only spiritually acceptable but also tribally acceptable because of their position within the clan. There are many obvious dangers ahead, not the least of which is the danger of trying to force such a system into a typically Caucasian mold. But we are convinced that this exciting path is nevertheless the path of the Spirit. For those of us who are not aboriginal and who have the privilege of sharing in this movement, it therefore truly becomes a matter of "God's power and human imagination." Aboriginal Christians of course need no imagination to work in a way that is perfectly natural to them, although they need the imagination to work among the part-aboriginals. It is we of other races who need the imagination to see that it is indeed God working thus, and to avoid hindering his work by our preconceptions and our analysis of past history.

It is instructive to compare briefly the development among the aboriginals in North Australia with two of those other spiritual developments among very different peoples mentioned initially. For instance, the char-

ismatic renewal in Singapore, which has undoubtedly led to a great
outburst of evangelism, has not as yet significantly affected the Chinese-
speaking churches of Singapore. It has largely followed the lines of the
"English-educated" group, who are perhaps less culturally conditioned
than the vernacular churches and more open to influences, spiritual and
otherwise, from the larger world outside. This group is made up of
"Hellenists," not "Hebrews" (to use biblical language). It is also interesting to note that a generation ago, when John Sung, the gifted Chinese
evangelist, had a mighty harvest among the Chinese-speaking churches,
it affected the English-speaking churches only superficially. Both of
these cases seem to suggest that the initial impact of a spiritual movement
is largely restricted to its own cultural group (like the "Welsh Revival,"
for instance, in past history), but the constant prayer and desire of every
Christian is that it will not stop there. In the case of John Sung, a broader
effect was eventually felt: he had a later and secondary impact on some
English-speaking churches, although one neither as universal nor as deep
as the impact on the Chinese-speaking churches. Such instances prompt
me to think that what we are dealing with here is not a theological factor
but a cultural factor that must be reckoned with. Using the "homogeneous
unit" approach to evangelism may be initial wisdom, perhaps in some
cases initial necessity, but it should not be regarded as permanent.

The remarkable growth of "student churches," especially in parts of
East Asia, also illustrates both the opportunities and the perils of "homogeneous group evangelism" under the influence of a new spiritual stim-
ulus. Students can best evangelize students—that is self-evident from the
results. But ultimately a religious group consisting entirely of students is
not a Christian church but an enlarged Sunday school. God's ideal for the
church is the richness that comes from diversities of age, sex, status, and
culture comprehended within one body (1 Cor. 12:13).

The various kinds of "homogeneous group evangelism" here discussed are interim steps, means to reach the goal of one body "made up of
many parts." Perhaps they are temporary concessions to our human
weakness, yet undoubtedly they are used by the Spirit, as all recent
spiritual experience shows.

Appendix III

The East African Revival

Gresford Chitemo

The East African Revival came down from Uganda and reached Tanzania in 1939. From there it spread mainly in the evangelical section of the Anglican Church known as the Church Missionary Society—CMS.

One of the people who was caught up in the revival was Pastor Yohana Majani Omari. He was convicted by the Holy Spirit of superficial Christianity, hate, hypocrisy, and other sins, and he repented of all these errors. He had to be reconciled to his wife and to his congregation; he was broken before them, confessing many things to them.

Then the Holy Spirit filled the pastor's life, even though he did not speak in tongues, prophesy, or perform miracles. The Holy Spirit made his ministry very effective by using it to convict many people of sin and make them repent and turn to Christ in faith. God used Pastor Omari in Tanzania and East Africa and overseas to bring many into his Kingdom. For example, during my visit to Australia in March 1984, I met a few people who had received Christ through his ministry when he had visited there in 1958. Missionaries from Ireland, England, and Australia have expressed their gratitude to God for using this man to bring them to a saving knowledge of the Lord Jesus in their lives. Praise the Lord!

Although I was convicted by the Holy Spirit while reading the New Testament, by God's grace Pastor Omari was the instrument that God used to help me know the Lord better and to grow in my Christian life. When this man spoke, I felt as if a hand was touching my chest. I was not the only one who experienced this; many others felt the same thing.

In 1955 Pastor Omari became the first African bishop, the assistant to the bishop of Central Tanganyika. Through this office the Lord opened a very wide door for him to preach the gospel to almost all the Protestant denominations in Tanzania, despite strong opposition from some of the church leaders, including church leaders in the Diocese of Central Tanganyika. Others later joined Pastor Omari in his evangelistic efforts: two secondary school teachers from Uganda, some pastors who were touched by the Holy Spirit, and some lay evangelists whom God called.

In 1963 Pastor Omari was called to be with his Master. But after his death many people who were saved during the revival became witnesses for Jesus Christ. This helped the church to grow very quickly indeed. It was during this time that God called me to full-time ministry in the church. I thank God for the East African Revival, through which Jesus saved my soul.

The main characteristics of the East African Revival were these:

1. Openness in confession and repentance of sin.
2. Making restitution and reconciliation where relationships were broken. (I remember that many of the boys in the school where I was teaching used to ask each Saturday for permission to go back to the primary schools they had attended in order to put things right with their teachers.)
3. Brokenness (not insisting on one's own rights) and readiness to admit sin or fault when one's error was pointed out by a brother or a sister.
4. Meeting for fellowship—sharing testimonies, "walking in the light" (being completely honest and open about motives, intentions, and actions). When someone wanted to build a house or start a farm, he "walked in the light" so that all the brothers and sisters knew what was happening. Likewise, those who wanted to marry "walked in the light" regarding their engagement. We prayed and read God's Word together. Then one brother or sister spoke on the passage, and others shared how the passage had helped them. After that we prayed for matters that had been brought into the light.
5. Acceptance of evangelistic responsibility. Each believer knew that he or she had a responsibility to let Jesus be known to others. This was the way the gospel spread everywhere. One day in the bush, for example, I found some women collecting firewood, and one among them was telling the others about the Lord Jesus.

This revival is still going on today, and there are conventions everywhere—in parishes, in deaneries, and even in small churches. The aim is to strengthen those in the fellowship and to reach out to others and bring them to a living faith in the Lord. Through the East African Revival, which is the work of the Holy Spirit, the church is growing despite the fact that there are still many traditionalists, Muslims, and people of other religions like Hinduism and Buddhism—mainly immigrants from Asia or people of Asian origins. But we still need the prayers of brothers and sisters all over the world for the work of evangelism in Tanzania.

One day in 1973 I heard of Edmund John, a man of God who was the brother of Johnson Sepeku, then the archbishop of Tanzania. This man was being used by God to preach the gospel, and many were convicted and repented of their sins. He was also praying for those who had diseases, and they were being healed.

I went to see Edmund John to find out if he was indeed a man of God, or if he was one of those about whom the Lord Jesus had said, "Many will say to me on that day, 'Lord, Lord, did we not prophesy in your name, and in your name drive out demons and perform many miracles?' Then I will tell them plainly, 'I never knew you. Away from me, you evildoers!'"

When, at an open-air meeting, I heard about his conversion, about the time he spent with the Word of God and his experience with the Holy Spirit and the way Jesus Christ had spoken to him, I was impressed. I was impressed with the quality of his humility and the way he glorified the Lord Jesus and his saying that only Jesus is the healer. In my heart I was convinced that he had been with the Lord. This conviction is hard to put into words. The nearest I can come to describing it is to liken it to Elizabeth's experience when she met with Mary, the mother of Jesus Christ our Lord. Just as there were signs in her womb, there were signs in my heart.

After this meeting I asked Edmund John to come to our diocese in November 1973. Fasting, vigils, and faith healing had not been a part of the East African Revival, but that changed when Edmund John came to Berega. He ministered in the church from Sunday afternoon until Wednesday morning. We fasted from six o'clock in the morning until six o'clock in the evening. At that time all of us ate something except Reverend John, who neither ate nor drank anything. The pastors congregated in one room and prayed all night. A few of us stayed with Edmund and prayed with him during the night. We prayed every hour on the hour. We did not offer the usual prayers of supplication. We praised and thanked God for his blessings and the wonders of creation—hills and mountains, lakes, rivers, and seas, valleys and springs of water, animals, humankind, and so forth. You might think that these were childish expressions, but at the time it seemed as if a torch light was shining up to heaven. Edmund John called those expressions of thanks "greeting the Father."

After three days of fasting and three nights of prayer came the time of preaching. As we came out of the church, we heard people crying and saw them shaking with evil powers, and we could barely quiet them. We all preached in turns. Edmund John preached a very simple, straightforward sermon on salvation. He told the people that God offered the gift of healing as bait. People came to be healed of physical illness, but God wanted to save. The response to this sermon was good.

Then came the time to pray for the sick people. Edmund John said that we should start by praying for those people possessed by evil spirits because there were so many of them: when they entered the church, they filled three-quarters of it. Some were crying; others were rolling on the floor; some were speaking nonsense; a few were even reciting Scripture or singing Christian songs or hymns. Edmund prayed in the name of Jesus, the King of Kings, the most powerful name, and all were freed. Then a group with other diseases entered. The records in my diary show the following figures: on Wednesday, November 21, 503 entered the church, and 458 were healed; on Thursday, November 22, 304 entered, and 280 were healed; on Friday, November 23, 683 entered, and 567 were healed.

During the time of praying for the sick, the pastors and other brethren were kneeling in one section of the church, saturating the proceedings in prayer. On the third day, before he left, Edmund John asked three pastors to continue praying for the sick. (Unfortunately, I had an appointment in Nairobi, so I left before the work ended.) This was a real apprenticeship. The pastors prayed, and people were healed.

Since that time, pastors visit each diocese, deanery, and parish to minister to the sick and those who need spiritual power. Because the gospel preaching is accompanied by the work of the Holy Spirit and there are signs and wonders, the power in the name of the Lord is apparent. People come to be healed of diseases or freed of demons. After they are prayed for and healed, they are instructed and prepared for baptism.

This gospel with its signs and miracles has caused many—Muslims, traditional people, and nominal Christians—to believe in the saving power of our Lord. As my experience has shown, the work of the Holy Spirit is truly marvelous.

Appendix IV

Renewing the Worship of the Local Church

Philip LeFeuvre

This case study relates to a specialist ministry, that of a campus chaplaincy of a South African university, but the principles I observed operating in that context I have also seen and have myself applied in local congregational contexts as well.

From April 1973 until December 1976 I was the Anglican (Episcopalian) chaplain on a university campus. I inherited a group of twelve students who met each Sunday morning for a purely said liturgical Eucharist and met each Sunday evening to discuss a theological, sociopolitical, or other current topic, a discussion that began and ended with prayer. There was no emphasis on evangelism except on the part of two or three students who "were given to that sort of thing." My predecessor had been a godly and prayerful man whose ministry had tended to stress the individual pastoring of students with problems, the awakening of Christian responsibility in the oppressive context of South African racialism, and the maintaining of statutory services.

My own philosophy of ministry was different. I stressed worship, evangelism, and discipleship. These were to be achieved by prayer and a ministry carried out by every member and based on the use of gifts in the community of the body. This case study does not require a description of the development of the total ministry but only a description of that which relates to worship and evangelism. Nevertheless, it should be noted that renewal of worship affects *every* aspect of congregational life and witness.

I began by learning what it is to take time to pray and to wait upon the Holy Spirit's leading—the two are by no means the same thing. Basically they represent the difference between talking and listening, and we really needed to listen. The outcome? We decided to place our emphasis on the Sunday evening service, and to turn it into a weekly Eucharist. I use the word "Eucharist" advisedly; the ministry of the Word and the breaking of bread had to occur in and give rise to a context of heartfelt and genuine thanksgiving and praise.

We were fortunate in being able to use a new liturgical form that gave shape and substance to our worship but also allowed for three important things: extemporary prayer and singing at a number of significant points in the service (e.g., after the Scripture readings and/or sermon, during and after the receiving of the bread and wine, etc.), the maximum use of gifts (e.g., healing, speaking in tongues, prophecy, etc.), and maximum participation by the laity (e.g., as leaders of worship, readers, possessors of special gifts, etc.). It did not take us long to discover the vital role of music and song in our worship. Music could be employed in a variety of forms: conventional hymns (sung at a good pace where appropriate!), choruses, spontaneous singing, singing in tongues, solos or duets, instrumental interludes, small choir pieces. Intelligently, beautifully, and often spontaneously used, music really lifted us in worship into the heavens. The liturgy should be similarly employed, we realized. It is possible to kill it stone dead by rattling it off like a parrot. It is also possible to make it come to life by using it intelligently, in a real spirit of worship, in the recognition of its beauty and of the freedom it permits. We worked to make the music and the liturgy all that they can be, and thus our worship became eucharistic, liturgical, musical, and permitted the spontaneous and individual contribution of each worshiper.

Certain forms of ecclesiastical architecture occasionally pose difficulties for spontaneous and individual contributions. Nevertheless, I have seen a number of parishes and congregations who, after seeking the mind of the Holy Spirit concerning their local situation, have successfully applied the basic pattern I have outlined. There are several results, usually very similar to those we experienced on the university campus:

1. a real sense of the presence of God, loving in creation, loving in redemption, holy and making holy, worthy to be praised, transforming to be known.
2. the creation of a new dynamic and depth of fellowship. For most, this went beyond happy smiles and chatter in an atmosphere of spiritual

euphoria. It spilled over into witness on the campus as individuals began to discover their gifts and the freedom of the Holy Spirit to use them. Thus evangelists discovered that they *were* evangelists and started to evangelize. Similarly, there were those who could disciple new Christians, those who could lead small groups in university residences, those who became involved in the politically active organizations on campus, and those with gifts of counseling, encouragement, and personal ministry. The exercise of these gifts, of course, was stimulated not only by the nature of the worship itself but by the ongoing teaching that took place within it. And these gifts were not exercised independently or autonomously but in relation to the worshiping community and under the guidance of its leadership.

3. a sense of enjoyment. This is neither trite nor superficial. It is the Lord's intention that worshiping him should lift up the spirit and gladden the heart—and so it does.

This kind of worship produced, among other things, growth and evangelism. Some came to worship because they heard about the services and enjoyed them once they began attending; some were brought along by others; some were converted in the student residences and came as a result; some came asking questions; some came with personal needs. Many were converted during the services, not always as a result of direct appeal. True, some conversions were the result of an appeal from a preacher or a fellow student in conversation. But often conversions were a response to a sense of God's presence in the service or to increasing involvement in and with the body of Christ. Sometimes such conversions were gradual. Whatever their description, they took place a decade ago, and most of them have stood the test of time.

The vast majority of the students of those days with whom I am still in contact are today walking with the Lord, but I also have to note that there have been casualties. Some of these I think I could have foretold. There were those, for example, who enjoyed and were very involved in worship but were reluctant to be involved in obedient, self-sacrificing discipleship. Perhaps this commitment is an acid test. However, one or two leaders are no longer walking with the Lord, and to me this is a mystery.

Despite such casualties, my university experience and the successful application of the "campus" principles in parish and congregational situations have convinced me that there is a strong correlation between renewed spiritual worship and evangelism, and that both, to be genuine, must be inspired, motivated, and led by the Holy Spirit. The starting

point is prayer and waiting on the Lord, speaking and listening, but
especially listening.

This case study is set in a South African context, and for most people
mention of South Africa will correctly suggest discrimination, injustice,
and monumental insensitivity to human dignity. I therefore feel it appropriate to elaborate my earlier assertion that "this kind of worship produced, *among other things,* growth and evangelism."

As a result of some of the spontaneous prayers offered during worship,
a number of students approached me to set up a seminar on Christian
responsibility in the South African context. The university was a so-
called "white university," and although some of the students were already
politicized, others felt themselves to be ignorant in this area, especially in
terms of their Christian discipleship. It is significant that this desire to be
better informed arose out of a worship context.

The seminar drew about eighty students, who met weekly for two
years. Since that time, five of them have served prison sentences (two for
fairly lengthy periods), mainly for refusing to defend the apartheid system militarily or to prolong the South African occupation of Namibia.
The seminar was still being held when the Soweto riots of 1976 broke out.
I concluded my ministry on that campus praising God that Christian
students took practical initiatives to organize themselves and fellow students to get into the townships, to meet the needs of suffering people, and
to register the strongest protests against police brutality.

Appendix V

The Power of Evangelistic Bible Studies

Ada Lum

An interchurch magazine in the Philippines reported the following:

> Last year Pastor Camacho baptized 60 converts out of six home Bible studies. Pastor Camacho said he and his wife conduct six evangelistic home Bible studies a week. The average attendance in each Bible study is ten. This means they are witnessing to more than 60 a month.
>
> Comparing the cost of their involvement in a recent public evangelistic crusade and [the cost of] their home Bible studies, Pastor Camacho revealed that his church gave a thousand *pesos* to the ten-day crusade, but profited only three converts. On the other hand, he and his wife do not spend more than one hundred *pesos* to conduct Bible studies. Yet the profit is so much more in terms of adding new members.
>
> Nevertheless, Pastor Camacho still uses the mass evangelism approach despite the low yield of the follow-up.

Our Filipino brother is following the example of the early apostles in using both public proclamation of the gospel and small-group evangelism. We are familiar with the great apostolic preaching of Peter, Paul, and others in Acts. But some of us may not be aware that countless home Bible studies, both evangelistic and pastoral groups, were frequently held (Acts 2:46-47; 5:42; 10:24; 18:7; 20:20). Specific examples of such personal investigation of the Scriptures include those of Philip with the Ethiopian official (Acts 8:26-40), Paul with the Berean Jews (Acts 17:10-12), and Priscilla and Aquila with the Grecian Apollos (Acts 18:24-28).

In our international student ministry we encourage all valid means of evangelism. Yet on every continent we constantly find that the most common effective means is the evangelistic Bible study. Often it is the complement of the more general, extensive kind of evangelism as preparation or follow-through. Usually it is the quiet, ongoing work of the fellowship in reaching out to the people around them with the message of Jesus. This is especially true where open evangelism is illegal—which is probably the case in at least half the countries in the world. But in all countries "Bible study" also describes situations where nonreligious people have no desire to go to a local church but are open to discuss religious issues objectively in an informal setting. In addition, it also applies to contexts in which religious people are still dissatisfied and seeking meaning in their lives and greater spiritual reality.

An evangelistic Bible study personally introduces seekers to Jesus Christ through well-selected Bible passages that are studied objectively in a friendly atmosphere. Some Filipinos call such meetings "discussion groups." Many North Americans refer to them as "investigative Bible studies." The Swedish like to use the phrase "open Bible studies." On the other hand, some Africans and Japanese want to be straightforward and call the gatherings "evangelistic Bible studies" so that their friends who attend will know what to expect! In any case, all who hold these meetings are seeking to follow the apostolic example of Philip, who, following the Spirit's leading, listened to the Ethiopian official's question about the biblical passage he was reading, and then "began with that very passage of Scripture and told him [the Ethiopian official] the good news about Jesus" (Acts 8:26-40).

I can draw on personal experience to illustrate the effectiveness of evangelistic Bible study. The largest evangelistic student fellowship in the world is not in the United States or the United Kingdom. It is in Singapore, where Buddhism predominates. In the early 1970s, when I was invited to help train students at the University of Singapore in evangelistic Bible studies, the Varsity Christian Fellowship there had about 160 members. They were divided into twenty Bible study groups of seven or eight participants. VCF was known as the largest and liveliest organization on that campus of 10,000 students.

But the student leaders of the group were dissatisfied with the fact that each year only ten to fifteen people were being converted to Christ. In considering these small numbers, they realized that their outreach had been too dependent on a few "experienced" evangelists. So they further divided the twenty Bible study groups into forty smaller groups of four people each, giving them a neutral-sounding but significant name—contact groups. These contact groups met regularly for mutual encouragement through study discussions and prayer, but they also worked together to contact outsiders. The fellowship also continued to have its large meetings with systematic Bible exposition led by experienced teachers. At the end of that year the fellowship had doubled its membership.

The next year the fellowship began with about 75 contact groups. At the end of that second year the fellowship had again doubled—to 600 members. In the third year their growth apparently slowed; still, they had about 900 members. Today, in the mid-eighties, the group numbers over 1800, with 60 percent of the medical faculty (department) involved in Christian life and witness.

The university graduates who participated in VCF have gone on to make a concrete impact on the churches in Singapore and Malaysia. They have been providing biblical leadership and ongoing evangelistic outreach in their communities.

On a much wider scale, the amazing story of God's church in China during the thirty years of Maoist revolution illustrates the same kind of growth. Stripped of all missionary props, religious freedom, and traditional church leadership, the believers did the instinctive thing. They met in small groups anywhere they could—in their homes or in the fields. These times of worship and mutual exhortation often focused on a single page of the Bible passed from group to group. Yet not only were believers sustained, but countless others were added to the Lord.

Closer to home, my own local church in the last six years has helped to plant many new churches outside of Honolulu. All of these began as friendly, loving, evangelistic Bible studies held in the homes of Christian lay people or sometimes in the homes of those seeking instruction.

In Hawaii, for friends to "talk story" means to discuss experiences and opinions on a topic in a highly relaxed atmosphere. In "talk story evangelism" we encourage the seeker to tell his story of whatever he has experienced or thought about God. It doesn't matter how negative or sub-biblical his story may seem to us. It's *his* story, and it is important to him. We try to be sensitive and alert, trusting the Lord to remind us of a gospel story that can merge with the seeker's story.

My own parents came to know the Lord in this way. But in their case it took several months of daily studying of the gospel. They were both in their seventies. For decades Mother had been a traditional ancestor worshiper, and Father, a typical Confucian agnostic.

What all these stories have in common is that the seekers (and they did not always realize they were seekers) had a chance to take a firsthand look at Jesus in the Scriptures, to respond to the passage and discuss it with friends, and to express their doubts and questions in an accepting atmosphere. When this kind of climate exists, evangelism can occur in any kind of Bible study.

Bibliography

Alexander, John W., ed. *Confessing Christ as Lord: The Urbana 81 Compendium.* Downers Grove, Ill.: InterVarsity Press, 1982.

Allen, Roland. *Pentecost and the World: The Revelation of the Holy Spirit in the "Acts of the Apostles."* London: Oxford University Press, 1917.

Bannerman, James. *The Church of Christ.* 2 vols. Edinburgh: T. & T. Clark, 1887.

Barclay, William. *The Promise of the Spirit.* Philadelphia: Westminster Press, 1960.

Bavinck, J. H. *The Impact of Christianity on the Non-Christian World.* Grand Rapids: Eerdmans, 1948.

_____. *Inleiding in de Zendingswetenschap.* Kampen: J. H. Kok, 1954.

Beasley-Murray, G. R. "Jesus and the Spirit." *Mélanges Bibliques en hommage au R. P. Béda Rigaux.* Ed. A. Descamps and A. de Halleux. Gembloux: Duculot, 1970.

Berkouwer, G. C. *The Church.* Trans. J. E. Davison. Studies in Dogmatics Series. Grand Rapids: Eerdmans, 1976.

_____. *Faith and Justification.* Trans. Lewis Smedes. Studies in Dogmatics Series. Grand Rapids: Eerdmans, 1954.

_____. *The Sacraments.* Trans. Hugo Bekker. Studies in Dogmatics Series. Grand Rapids: Eerdmans, 1969.

Beyerhaus, Peter. *Die Selbstandigkeit der jungen Kirchen als missionarisches Problem.* Wuppertal-Barmen: Verlag der Rheinischen Missions-Gesellschaft, 1956.

Blocher, Henri. *La doctrine du péché et de la rédemption.* 3 vols. Vaux-sur-Seine: Faculté Libre de Théologie Evangélique, 1982.

Bloesch, Donald. *The Christian Life and Salvation.* Grand Rapids: Eerdmans, 1967.

Bluck, John. *Beyond Technology.* Geneva: World Council of Churches, 1984.

Boer, Harry R. *Pentecost and Missions.* Grand Rapids: Eerdmans, 1961.

Bruner, Frederick Dale. *A Theology of the Holy Spirit: The Pentecostal Experience and the New Testament Witness.* Grand Rapids: Eerdmans, 1970.

Buchanan, James. *The Doctrine of Justification: An Outline of Its History in the Church and of Its Exposition from Scripture.* London: Banner of Truth Trust, 1961.

_____. *The Office and Work of the Holy Spirit.* Carlisle, Pa.: Banner of Truth Trust, 1984.

Candlish, James S. *The Christian Salvation: Lectures on the Work of Christ, Its Appropriation and Its Issues.* Edinburgh: T. & T. Clark, 1899.

Canon, William R. *The Theology of John Wesley with Special Reference to the Doctrine of Justification.* New York: Abingdon-Cokesbury Press, 1946.

Carter, Charles W. *The Person and Ministry of the Holy Spirit: A Wesleyan Perspective.* Grand Rapids: Baker Book House, 1974.

Citron, Bernhard. *New Birth: A Study of the Evangelical Doctrine of Conversion in the Protestant Fathers.* Edinburgh: Edinburgh University Press, 1951.

Conn, Harvie, ed. *Theological Perspectives on Church Growth.* Nutley, N.J.: Presbyterian and Reformed Publishing Company, 1976.

Cook, Harold R. *An Introduction to the Study of Christian Missions.* Chicago: Moody Press, 1954.

Cullmann, Oscar. "Eschatology and Missions in the New Testament." In *The Background of the New Testament and Its Eschatology.* Ed. W. D. Davies and D. Daube. Cambridge: Cambridge University Press, 1956. Pp. 409-27.

————, and F. J. Leenhart. *Essays on the Lord's Supper.* Trans. J. C. Davies. Richmond: John Knox Press, 1958.

Douglas, J. D., ed. *Let the Earth Hear His Voice.* Minneapolis: World Wide Publications, 1975.

Engel, James F. *Contemporary Christian Communications.* Nashville: Thomas Nelson, 1979.

————, and Wilber Norton. *What's Gone Wrong with the Harvest?* Grand Rapids: Zondervan, 1975.

Gilhuis, J. C. *Ecclesiocentrische Aspecten van het Zendingswerk.* Kampen: J. H. Kok, 1955.

Goodwin, Thomas. *The Work of the Holy Spirit in Our Salvation.* Edinburgh: Banner of Truth Trust, 1979.

Gordon, A. J. *The Holy Spirit in Missions—Student Mission Power: Report of the First International Convention of the Student Volunteer Movement for Foreign Missions.* New York: Revell, 1893.

————. *The Ministry of the Spirit.* Philadelphia: Judson Press, 1949.

Green, Michael. *I Believe in the Holy Spirit.* Grand Rapids: Eerdmans, 1975.

Hahn, Ferdinand. *Mission in the New Testament.* London: SCM Press, 1965.

Hendry, George S. *The Holy Spirit in Christian Theology.* London: SCM Press, 1957.

Hesselgrave, David J. *Communicating Christ Cross-Culturally.* Grand Rapids: Zondervan, 1978.

Hodges, M. L. *A Theology of the Church and Its Mission.* Springfield, Mo.: Gospel Publishing House, 1977.

Howard, David M. *By the Power of the Holy Spirit.* Downers Grove, Ill.: Inter-Varsity Press, 1973.

Hull, J. H. E. *The Holy Spirit in the Acts of the Apostles.* London: Lutterworth, 1967.

Inch, Morris A. *Saga of the Spirit: A Biblical, Systematic and Historical Theology of the Holy Spirit*. Grand Rapids: Baker Book House, 1985.

Jay, Eric George. *The Church: Its Changing Image Through Twenty Centuries*. 2 vols. London: SPCK, 1977-78.

Kalilombe, Patrick. "Evangelization and the Holy Spirit." *African Ecclesiastical Review* 78 (1976): 8-78.

Kane, J. Herbert. *Christian Missions in Biblical Perspective*. Grand Rapids: Baker Book House, 1976.

Kinlaw, Dennis F. *Preaching in the Spirit*. Grand Rapids: Francis Asbury Press, 1985.

Kraft, Charles H. *Communication Theory for Christian Witness*. Nashville: Abingdon Press, 1983.

Kromminga, John. *All One Body We: The Doctrine of the Church in Ecumenical Perspective*. Grand Rapids: Eerdmans, 1970.

Kuyper, Abraham. *The Work of the Holy Spirit*. Trans. Henri De Vries. Grand Rapids: Eerdmans, 1973.

Kydd, Ronald A. N. *Charismatic Gifts in the Early Church*. Peabody, Mass.: Hendrickson, 1984.

Ladd, George. *The Blessed Hope: A Biblical Study of the Second Advent and the Rapture*. Grand Rapids: Eerdmans, 1956.

———. *Crucial Questions about the Kingdom of God*. Grand Rapids: Eerdmans, 1952.

———. *The Gospel of the Kingdom: Scriptural Studies in the Kingdom of God*. Grand Rapids: Eerdmans, 1959.

———. *The Presence of the Future: The Eschatology of Biblical Realism*. Grand Rapids: Eerdmans, 1974.

Lindsell, Harold. *An Evangelical Theology of Missions*. Grand Rapids: Zondervan Publishing House, 1970.

Lourdusamy, D. Simon. "The Holy Spirit and the Missionary Action in the Church." In *Prospettive di Missiologia*, Oggi. Documenta Missionali 16. Rome: Universita Gregoriana Editrice, 1982. Pp. 46-58.

MacGregor, Geddes. *Corpus Christi: The Nature of the Church According to Reformed Tradition*. Philadelphia: Westminster Press, 1958.

McLeish, Alexander. *The Priority of the Holy Spirit in Christian Witness*. London: World Dominion Press, 1967.

Martin, David, and Peter Mullen, eds. *Strange Gifts?* Oxford: Basil Blackwell, 1984.

Minear, Paul S. *Images of the Church in the New Testament*. Philadelphia: Westminster Press, 1960.

Moody, Dale. "The Holy Spirit and Missions: Vision and Dynamic." *Review and Expositor* 62 (1965): 75-81.

Mott, John R. *The Evangelization of the World in This Generation*. New York: Student Volunteer Movement Press, 1900.

Moule, C. F. D. *The Holy Spirit*. Grand Rapids: Eerdmans, 1979.

Murray, Iain. *The Puritan Hope*. London: Banner of Truth Trust, 1971.

Murray, John. *Redemption—Accomplished and Applied*. Grand Rapids: Eerdmans, 1955.

Newbigin, Lesslie. *The Open Secret: Sketches for a Missionary Theology*. London: SPCK, 1978.

————. *The Relevance of Trinitarian Doctrine for Today's Mission*. London: Edinburgh House Press, 1963.

————. "The Work of the Holy Spirit in the Life of the Asian Churches." Paper presented at the East Asia Christian Conference (1959) at Kuala Lumpur, Malaya; and the John R. Mott Memorial Lectures, London, 1960.

Nicholls, Bruce J. *Contextualization: A Theology of Gospel and Culture*. Downers Grove, Ill.: InterVarsity Press, 1979.

Nida, Eugene. *Message and Mission*. South Pasadena, Calif.: William Carey Library, 1972.

Niles, Daniel T. *Upon the Earth: The Mission of God and the Missionary Enterprise of the Churches*. New York: McGraw-Hill, 1962.

————. "The Work of the Holy Spirit in the World." In *Christian Mission in Theological Perspective*. Nashville: G. K. Anderson, 1959.

Pache, René. *The Person and Work of the Holy Spirit*. Trans. J. D. Emerson. London: Marshall, Morgan & Scott, 1956.

Packer, J. I. *Evangelism and the Sovereignty of God*. Downers Grove, Ill.: InterVarsity Press, 1961.

————. *Keep in Step with the Spirit*. New York: Revell, 1984.

Peters, G. W. *A Theology of Church Growth*. Grand Rapids: Zondervan, 1981.

Poulton, John. *The Christian Communicator's Questions*. London: WACC, 1960.

Ramm, Bernard. *The Witness of the Spirit: An Essay on the Contemporary Relevance of the Internal Witness of the Holy Spirit*. Grand Rapids: Eerdmans, 1960.

Ranson, C. W., ed. *Renewal and Advance*. London: Edinburgh House Press, 1948.

Ridderbos, Herman. *The Coming of the Kingdom*. Trans. H. De Jongste. Philadelphia: Presbyterian and Reformed Publishing Company, 1969.

Samuel, Vinay, and Chris Sugden, eds. *Sharing Jesus in the Two Thirds World*. Grand Rapids: Eerdmans, 1984.

Schweizer, Eduard. "The Spirit of Power: The Uniformity and Diversity of the Concept of the Holy Spirit in the New Testament." Trans. John Bright and Eugene Debor. *Interpretation* 6 (1952): 259-78.

Seamands, John T. "The Role of the Holy Spirit in Church Growth." In *God, Man, and Church Growth*. Ed. A. R. Tippett. Grand Rapids: Eerdmans, 1973.

Seumois, André. "The Holy Spirit and Missionary Dynamism." *Omnis Terra* (Roma) 14 (1980): 232-48.

Smeaton, George. *The Doctrine of the Holy Spirit*. Edinburgh: Banner of Truth Trust, 1974.

Smedes, Lewis B. *All Things Made New: A Theology of Man's Union with Christ*. Grand Rapids: Eerdmans, 1970.

Smith, Eugene L. *God's Mission and Ours*. New York: Abingdon Press, 1961.

Speer, Robert E. *Missionary Principles and Practice*. New York: Revell, 1902.

Starkey, Lycurgus Monroe. *The Work of the Holy Spirit*. New York: Abingdon Press, 1962.

Stibbs, Alan. *God's Church: A Study in the Biblical Doctrine of the People of God*. London: Inter-Varsity Press, 1959.

————. *Sacrament, Sacrifice and Eucharist: The Meaning, Function and Use of the Lord's Supper*. London: Tyndale Press, 1962.

Stott, John. *Christian Mission in the Modern World*. Downers Grove, Ill.: Inter-Varsity Press, 1975.

Stronstad, Roger. *The Charismatic Theology of St. Luke*. Peabody, Mass.: Hendrickson, 1984.

Swete, Henry Barclay. *The Holy Spirit in the New Testament: A Study of Primitive Christian Teaching*. London: Macmillan, 1910.

Taylor, John V. *The Go-Between God: The Holy Spirit and Christian Missions*. London: SCM Press, 1975.

Teng, Philip. "Mission—and the Church's Endowment." In *The Church's Worldwide Mission*. Ed. Harold Lindsell. Waco, Tex.: Word Books, 1966.

Thomas, W. H. G. *The Holy Spirit of God*. Grand Rapids: Eerdmans, 1955.

Tippett, Alan R. *Church Growth and the Word of God*. Grand Rapids: Eerdmans, 1970.

Verkuyl, J. *Contemporary Missiology: An Introduction*. Trans. and ed. Dale Cooper. Grand Rapids: Eerdmans, 1978.

Wells, David F. *Search for Salvation*. Downers Grove, Ill.: InterVarsity Press, 1974.

Wijngaards, J. N. M. "Witness of the Spirit in Evangelisation." In *Service and Salvation*. Nagpur Theological Conference on Evangelisation. Ed. J. Pathra-Pankal. Bangalore: Theological Publications in India, 1973.

Winslow, Octavius. *Personal Declension and Revival of Religion in the Soul*. Edinburgh: Banner of Truth Trust, 1978.

Wood, Leon J. *The Holy Spirit in the Old Testament*. Grand Rapids: Zondervan, 1976.

Yates, J. E. *The Spirit and the Kingdom*. London: SPCK, 1963.

Zopfi, Jakob. . . . *auf alles Fleisch*. Kreuzlingen, Switzerland: Dynamis Verlag, 1985.

Zwemer, Samuel. *Christianity: The Final Religion*. Grand Rapids: Eerdmans-Sevensma, 1920.